MW01201443

TRAINING BIRD DOGS

— WITH RONNIE SMITH KENNELS —

Proven Techniques and an Upland Tradition

TRAINING BIRD DOGS

WITH RONNIE SMITH KENNELS

Proven Techniques and an Upland Tradition

Reid Bryant with Ronnie Smith and Susanna Love
Photography by Brian Grossenbacher
With foreword by former Secretary of State James A. Baker III

UNIVERSE   ORVIS

This book is dedicated to Delmar Smith and Ronnie Smith, Sr.,
whose love of dogs became a family legacy.

CONTENTS

James A. Baker, III, the 61st U.S. Secretary of State, often says that while politics and public service are his vocation, hunting is his avocation.

T hey had buried him under our elm tree, they said—yet this was not totally true. For he really lay buried in my heart.

—Willie Morris, *My Dog Skip*

//

My dog Josh is buried in South Texas, behind our old house at Rockpile Ranch a few miles outside of Pearsall. That's a fitting final resting place for this English cocker spaniel because Josh was always happiest when he was in a part of the world where he could hunt quail or dove. Hunting, of course, was what he did best.

A stud-muffin with a burnt orange coat, sturdy body, and intelligent eyes, Josh was a tireless retriever who never gave up on a downed bird. Regardless of the height of the grass or the density of the prickly pear cactus, Josh remained vigilant until he found his prey—with his tail happily wagging all the while.

Unlike many of his brethren in the breed, Josh learned over time to become more than just a superb retriever. He learned to point live quail. I never figured out how he knew the difference between a live bird and a wounded one. But everyone who hunted behind Josh knew to get ready to shoot when he stopped and pointed.

Yes, my merry hunter was happiest when he was quartering the field, finding coveys, and softly dropping dead quail in my hand. And I was always happy when I was with him.

I've never trained a bird dog. But I've hunted with many of them, enough to know the qualities that make a good one. Successful bird dogs display a unique blend of obedience and independence, something that allows them to follow commands while also trusting their instincts. They have the intelligence required to become proficient at what they do and the stamina to run long distances and weather extreme conditions. And they have a fearlessness that allows them to explore an environment that often contains

rattlesnakes, javelinas, and other cantankerous predators. Hunting with these dogs is pure joy—one that links man with nature and transforms the hunt into a team sport.

Great bird dogs like Josh, however, have all those qualities and something extra. They have a naturally calm temperament that allows them to also be wonderful companions.

Josh was special, as comfortable sleeping peacefully on the floor next to my bed at night—or watching me eat breakfast—as he was digging through the hardscrabble South Texas underbrush looking for a bird. He liked my attention when I rubbed his ear, but he never demanded it. And he was my gentle friend.

Josh and I hunted together until he was 14 years old. He died a year later. Before then, I had already made plans to pass along his genes to other dogs. And so, I've been able to hunt with Little Josh and Josh Junior—good hunters both, but not quite equals of their father.

I've been fortunate during my 89 years on this earth to have had long and fulfilling friendships. President George H.W. Bush was the big brother I never had. I had three wonderful roommates in college, and all of us remain alive and close today. And God has blessed me with two loving wives—Mary Stuart Baker and Susan Garrett Baker—whose support, friendship, and love I will always cherish.

As for Josh, he was more than a just bird dog. He was one of my very best companions—ever.

A plaque I have inside the old house at Rockpile Ranch where Josh is buried reads:

Josh Baker
Faithful Friend
1995–2010

Those simple words cannot fully express what he meant to me.

While he may be in the ground, Josh will always be on my mind . . . and in my heart.

—*James A. Baker, III*

INTRODUCTION

T*he jagged blue ridges of the Belt Mountains* rise above the burnished gold pasture and wheat fields that surround our fall training camp. A flock of crows flies overhead, punctuating the afternoon with their telltale calls. Two white-and-liver pointer puppies play in their pen and periodically look over at us, ready for their evening walk in the field.

Over the past few years, we have come to this sanctuary on a friend's ranch in the Montana prairies. The ranch sits roughly 15 miles from the nearest paved road, nestled between dramatic coulees on the east and northwest sides. It offers expansive vistas and a terrific wild-bird habitat. A combination of grassland, steep coulees, and crop ground sustains healthy populations of Hungarian partridge and sharp-tailed grouse. This ranch is affectionately known as the Dirt Road Ranch.

My husband, Ronnie Smith, and I look over at the pointer puppies again and discuss their personalities. The larger liver pup has a thin blaze on his face and liver ticking developing on his legs and feet. Our kids have affectionately named him Rock, and the name suits the big-boned, even-keeled pup. His sister is lying almost completely on top of him, soaking up the afternoon sun. She is similar in build, but slightly smaller, and more physically refined than her male counterpart. She has a liver spot interrupting the thin blaze on her head and a large defining spot on her back. Being a little bit smaller, she is also quicker than Rock, and she tends to beat him to the punch in most matters of interest. Her name, Grace, is a nod to her great-great-grandmother, an elegant white-and-black pointer who died well before she was able to take her due position as the top hand on our string. The original Grace, however, left a significant impact on our line of bird dogs: She had one litter of pups in her lifetime, and the dogs in that single litter shaped our hunting string for years. Ronnie and I certainly hope a little bit of the old Grace shines through in this new generation.

Our journey with Rock and Grace has barely just begun. We will devote a lot of time and training over the next two years to develop and mature the pups into proficient bird finders. The cold north breeze chills our backs as we sit atop our hunting rig and discuss their development. We will spend the remainder of this month here at our northern camp, where we will do our best to ensure that the pups encounter as many birds as possible. Though the prairies of the Dirt Road Ranch are rich in birds and the lineage of the pups is rich in potential, we will keep our expectations realistic. All bird-dog prospects start somewhere, and the most important factor right now is that we maximize the experience and the education they gain from their time in these fields. Indeed, they may chase grasshoppers as a covey gets up, undetected, just in front of them, but that is part of the fun and the natural development process for all pups.

It is, after all, what we live for: the excitement and hope that stirs in us as we look forward to the coming chapters, in which we will experience and celebrate an enduring tradition of fine bird dogs.

With opportunity, time, and maturity, they will get better and better.

Next month, when the pups are four months old, we will take them with us to Texas for the quail season. When we are not running hunts with our seasoned dogs, we will get the pups to contact as many wild bobwhite quail as possible. In the spring, we will return to our home in Oklahoma and introduce the pups to pigeons, concentrating on building their prey drive to a pinnacle with steady bird exposure. When the pups are mature enough and their prey drive is at its peak, we will place them in our Basic Formal Training Class. There, they will gain the manners they will need to be proficient bird dogs and solid canine citizens. After their basic training is in place, we will return to the wheat fields and coulees of Montana to transition them from pen-raised birds to wild sharp-tailed grouse, Hungarian partridge, and pheasants. Though they will still be rookie bird dogs, they will accompany us to the rolling plains of Texas once more to finish honing their skills as we guide hunts for wild bobwhites. This first full season is, in effect, a tryout. By the conclusion of the first season, we will know if the pups have what it takes to earn a permanent place on our string. It will take countless hours of socialization and development, but the result will be more than worth the effort.

Each year begins a new cycle with new bird dogs to develop and an expansive new world for them to explore. Similarly, each year arrives with the promise of new opportunities for me and Ronnie—each location in our tour of the country's remote upland habitats offers a new range of experiences. It's a parade of transitions that allow the pups to become more resilient, flexible, and stronger as individuals. Sitting here on this Montana evening, watching two puppies resting in the encroaching purple shadow of the Belt Mountains, it is wonderful to consider all that lies ahead. It is, after all, what we live for—the excitement and hope that stirs in us as we look forward to the coming chapters in which we will experience and celebrate an enduring tradition of fine bird dogs.

This book is a composite of the experiences that we have since shared with Rock and Grace—and literally thousands of bird dogs, trainers, and owners. As Ronnie and I sat down with our friend Reid Bryant to consider the information we wanted to cover in these pages, we marveled at the sheer volume of insights we hoped to share. There were myriad animal behaviors and responses, a rich family history, endless old stories, and countless nuanced anecdotes of training different dogs with particular traits. As we began to compile this material into one single book, we quickly realized there are not enough pages to share all the fantastic observations, wonderful responses, and surprising insights that bird dogs have shared with us. Thus, we began to pare down the material to the most critical and translatable information. In no way can this book possibly address all the individual recipes we have used to train dogs with both extraor-

dinary talents and issues; however, it does cover all of the basic principles required to effectively train the majority of dogs.

As we drafted this book, we wrestled with how to most efficiently communicate all that we have learned. For the sake of clarity, simplicity, and continuity, we chose to use masculine pronouns when *generally* referencing dogs throughout the book. In *no way* does this have any bearing on how we feel about female trainers, female owners, or female dogs!

If you love upland hunting dogs and want to train them, this book will give you the structure and lessons necessary to maximize the potential of your functional, well-adjusted bird dog. Keep in mind that a large part of training—and a large part of a dog's performance—is determined by the individual relationships we cultivate with them. As owners, trainers, and hunters, we should never stop striving to better our relationships with our animals.

As students of animal behavior, Ronnie and I grew up, both in rural settings, studying the handling techniques of legendary horsemen, cattlemen, and handlers of wildlife. From Professor Beery to Ray Hunt and Tom Dorrance to Bud Williams, these folks spent untold hours with animals. If you have watched such trainers carefully, you will notice there is an economy of motion in everything they do with animals. These great trainers did not make unnecessary motions or noise; they exhibited a calm, quiet demeanor that conveyed purpose and direction. They had a deep understanding and empathy for the animals they worked with. They did not treat the animals as humans; to the contrary, they treated them as something special, unique, and revered. They were the true old whisperers of their time, and, even today, we can learn from their relationships with animals.

To successfully train dogs, never stop watching them and never stop learning from them. Pay attention to what they are telling you. The animals themselves are the true masters of teaching us how to best address their needs. This book can provide a basic structure and training format that works, but your animal will invariably tell you how to best apply it.

Susanna Love
Judith Basin County, Montana, 2017

Hughes
VINITA, OKLA.

HISTORY

Even as Susanna and I look forward to the development of the new pups who have yet to find a permanent place in our string, it is fascinating to reflect on how similar their life and training will be to that of the Smith dogs from the 1950s. In those early years of what has become a family legacy, my father, Ronnie Smith, Sr., and his brother, Delmar, implemented basic training on the prairies of Oklahoma. Each year, as the seasonal Oklahoma temperatures rose, Dad and Uncle Delmar packed up their families and a load of dogs and headed north to the Canadian prairie for a summer of training on wild birds.

Our family became a part of the local scenery in Estevan, Saskatchewan, in those years, arriving in the Canadian camp with dozens of potential gun dogs and field-trial prospects. Upon arrival, the Smith horses were rounded up from their winter grazing grounds and given quick refresher courses in handling, riding, and basic civility. Those horses designated to pull the wagon-load of dog boxes were harnessed and hitched for the first time in months, and the boxes were filled with pointers and setters and Brittanys. A commotion of barking dogs filled the sky of Central Canada as handlers on horseback led the wagon out across the prairie, dropping brace after brace of bird dogs to work their way into the day.

Ours is a family of storytellers, and all sorts of tall tales have been told and retold through the years, enough to become family legends. Several favorites have grown pretty colorful in the retelling, and now in his early 90s, Uncle Delmar still chuckles to remember how my cousin Mark quickly learned to get a good grip on the wagon seat when he saw his dad head out to flush a pointed bird and shoot the training gun. Even as a toddler, Mark had the good sense to know that the Canadian horses had not been worked since the past summer, and there was no guarantee that they would stand through the report of the shotgun. Every shot posed the strong possibility of a runaway by the team of horses until much later in the summer, when, nearing the end of the training season, the team would finally become

OPENING SPREAD: The Smith brothers, clockwise from top left: Milton, Lewis, Norbert, Ronnie, and Delmar **ABOVE**: Training in Canada during the summer of 1961, Roberta "Bobbie" Smith (wife of Ronnie Smith, Sr. handling dog wagon and team of horses **RIGHT**: Ronnie Smith, Jr., today

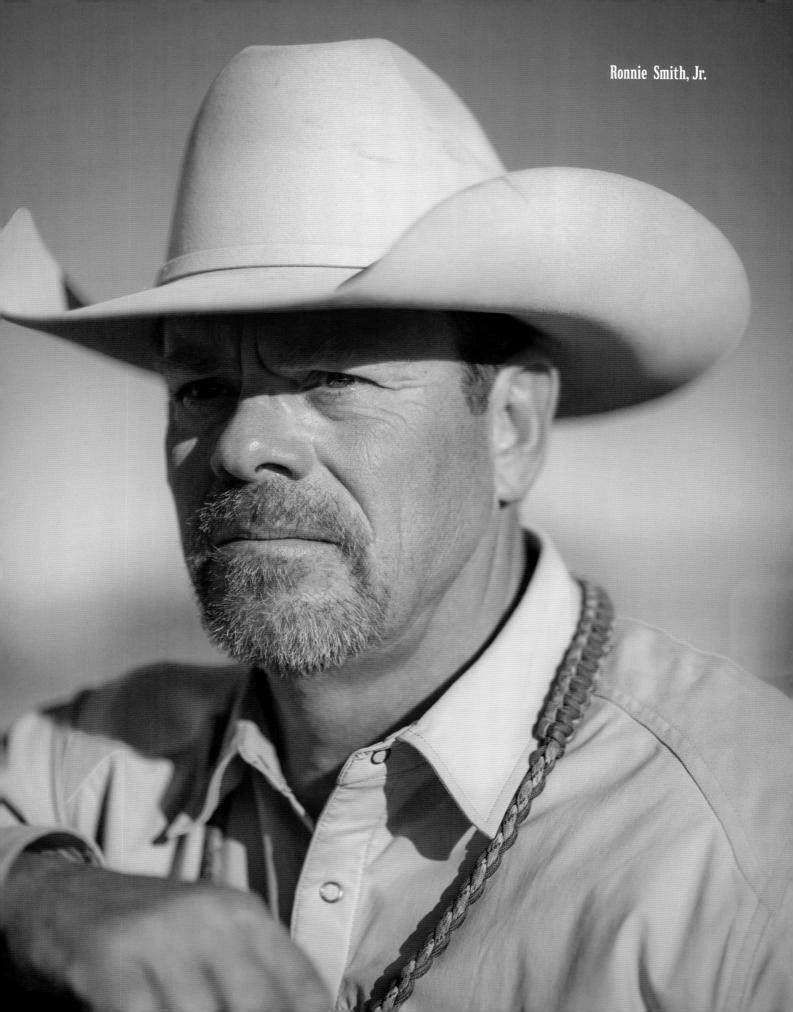
Ronnie Smith, Jr.

ABOVE: Rick Smith with award-winning Brittany, Pacolet Cheyenne Sam, and his trophies (from left to right)—the US Open Brittany Championship, the National Specialty Brittany Show, and the 1971 National Brittany Championship. RIGHT: At the 1973 International Endurance Open Shooting Dog Championship, Rick Smith holds award-winning Brittany CH. Pacolet Cheyenne Sam; Delmar and Tom Smith (third and fourth from left) and Ronnie Smith, Sr. (third from right).

somewhat conditioned to the noise.

Even though these tales of a life in bird dogs make for a story of their own, there is also a richer context that frames our family legacy within the world of pointing-dog training. That story begins in the tallgrass prairie country of the American South. In 1901, well before dad and Uncle Delmar ever tangled with a bird dog of any sort, Drs. J.C.W. Bland and Fred S. Clinton struck oil on a property of Creek Indian allotment near modern-day Red Fork, Oklahoma. Their first well, which was named Sue Bland #1, brought national attention to the territory around the frontier settlement of Tulsa. Back then, Oklahoma was still some years from statehood. In the decades before the turn of the century, the area had been parceled out into a patchwork—and some would say a throw-away—piece of prairie ground known as Indian Territory. Seen as lacking in prospects by the US government, the area had been given over to the displaced members of the Choctaw, Cherokee, Chickasaw, Creek, and Seminole nations, who'd been marched overland from their traditional homes on the more desirable ground to the south and east. The oil that was discovered in the land around Tulsa drew the interest of oil-hungry wildcatters, and in short order, a stream of both money and eastern businessmen in search of it cut a channel into what would become Oklahoma. As that wealth settled into the area and doubled itself, those new oil tycoons began to take notice of the region's abundance of native upland birds.

Through the early 1900s, Oklahoma's prairie chickens and bobwhite quail were in steady supply. The tallgrass prairie provided plenty of feed and cover, so the coveys were large and plentiful. These birds, which had long been considered little more than a sorry alternative to beefsteak by the locals, drew a good deal of interest from the eastern oilmen, who had hunted quail from horseback through the Black Belt of the American Southeast. In short order, both walking horses and pointing dogs joined the businessmen in their homes around Tulsa and Bartlesville, and as the wells sprung up and the money rolled in, a good deal of time and energy was spent exploring the bird cover around the growing cities. The newest residents of Oklahoma were more than happy to run their pointing dogs out in the allotment pastureland, following for miles on horseback and shooting a fair share of birds. For those with a nose for oil and a passion for bird dogs, Oklahoma proved a not-too-shabby place to hang a hat.

As the early years of the 20th Century wore on, Oklahoma's oil prospects grew and grew, as did the focus on dogs and horses. Seeing an opportunity, local farmers and ranchers from the eastern allotment lands turned their talents to the wants of the city sportsmen. Many Okie ranchers applied the

Delmar Smith

OPPOSITE: Delmar Smith, with 1960 National Brittany Champion Holiday Britt

knowledge they'd gained working ranch dogs, cutting horses, and roping horses to the tasks at hand, soon specializing as bird-dog handlers and horse trainers. Simultaneously, some noteworthy eastern bird-dog trainers began stopping through Eastern Oklahoma to run dogs and cool their heels, particularly around hunting and trial seasons. It was then, in that era when a gentleman still put a high priority on good dogs, good horses, and men known to have a steady hand with both, that my Uncle Delmar Smith began a legacy that would shape the future of bird dogs and bird-dog training.

No book about the Smith family training system would be complete without a tip of the hat in recognition of Uncle Delmar, who was in large part responsible for both getting the family started training bird dogs and for creating the bird-dog legacy that we remain so proud of. Like many of his kin, Delmar is a blue-eyed Cherokee whose skin is brown and leathery from long hours of work in the Oklahoma sun. Uncle Delmar was born in the Eastern Oklahoma town of Big Cabin in 1926. His father Fate, my grandfather, was also a registered member of the Cherokee

nation. Fate worked hard and squeezed a living out of the eastern prairie; he ran beef cattle on the outlying pastureland, leaning on his five sons to rise before dawn each morning to saddle their horses and to feed and check the cattle, rain or shine. Animals of all sorts were an important part of Delmar's childhood, and he was as fascinated by them then as he is today.

Uncle Delmar maintains that as a boy he would not allow any animal to come onto the Smith place without "contesting it," as he would either "ride it, rope it, or make a pet out of it." Delmar, alongside his younger brother, my father, Ronnie Sr., had a knack for catching and training—or "contesting"—coyotes, which he chased down on horseback and roped like he did the family's steers. He toted these coyotes, and

a variety of other critters, home to the Smith ranch (and his long-suffering mother), where he could look at them a little more closely. There were golden eagles, raccoons, sandhill cranes, hawks, and crows, all of which Delmar and Dad reared or rescued, satisfying an honest fascination with animal behavior that would never quit. As children, and even more so as adults, Uncle Delmar and Dad spent long hours just watching animals, studying their responses to environments, human contact, and stress. But that older generation of Smith boys, whether they admitted it or not, also had a real knack for reading people. Even today, as a man in his 90s, nothing makes Uncle Delmar's blue eyes twinkle more than sitting in someone's favorite chair, just to see how they respond.

Delmar and Dad's Oklahoma boyhood, rich as it was with creatures great and small, came about during a time when America afforded the crafts of horse training, dog training, and bird-dog trialing a great deal of respect. In that era, the oil boom had opened up an opportunity for men in Eastern Oklahoma to make a living out of training and handling dogs and horses. Eastern Oklahoma was a region that had been pretty hardscrabble for a lot of years, but when oil was found, those ranchers gifted with a steady and consistent hand with animals came to be in demand, and a new and honorable career was born. As mentioned above, many men turned their attention to bird dogs and riding horses as the wealthy folk around Tulsa became more eager to have the best of the best horses and dogs when hunting or trialing season came to pass. Eastern Oklahoma fast became a center for the bird-dog community and a regular stopover for a Who's Who of legendary trainers and handlers. Throughout Delmar and Dad's boyhood, men like Dutch Epperson, Jake Bishop, and Chesley Harris came to command a degree of fame, if not fortune, both in

Smith Family Training

From left: Tom Smith with Elhew Buckaroo, John Harvey with unknown dog, and Ronnie Smith, Sr., with Rip of Caddo

Delmar Smith stands behind his brother Ronnie Smith, Sr., who presents champion bird dog, Oklahoma Paladin Polly.

Ronnie Sr.'s first crew-cab dog truck, circa 1976

BELOW: Ronnie Smith, Sr., with champions
Rex of Caddo and Oklahoma Paladin Polly

DOG HANDLER, Ron Smith, Big Cabin, is shown at left with Storm Victor, first place winner in the open derby classic of the Arizona shooting dog championship and companion stakes, held recently in Kingman, Ariz. The dog is owned by Dr. C. A. Martin, Joplin, Mo. Second place went to Prejepa's I'm Meg, shown at center with its handler, Tom Smith, Ronnie's nephew. I'm Meg is owned by Jeanne and Preston Pate, also of Joplin, Mo. The third place winner, at right with handler Bob Soden, was Fonego Master Charge, owned by Steve Harris, Bakersfield, Calif.

B.C. dog handler wins
3 of 6 tests in West

Ronnie Smith, Big Cabin dog handler, has returned home from a 4,000 mile swing through the West with trophies acquired in two contests.

His dogs won three of the six they entered.

At his first stop, the Arizona shooting dog championship and companion stakes at Kingman, Ariz., Smith handled Man's Man for a first place in open puppy competition. Man's Man is owned by Dr. C. K. Doran, Tulsa.

In the open derby classic at Kingman, his Storm Victor also placed first. The dog is owned by J. R. Martin and Dr. C. A. Martin, Joplin, Mo.

Later at the open derby classic at Winnemucca, Nev., he won first place with Sports Page, owned by Bill Collie, Neosho, Mo. Man's Man was second in the open puppy classic there.

The area won a heavy share of the trophies offered at these two contests.

Prejepa's I'm Meg, owned by Jeanne and Preston Pate, Joplin, Mo., and handled by Ronnie Smith's nephew, Tom Smith, was second in the open derby classic at Kingman. Tom had a third in Winnemucca's open derby classic with Johnny Squire, owned by Bob Gibson, Jonesboro, Ark.

The Arizona run was held in the desert on chuckars. Storm Victor had four fines in 30 minutes there.

ABOVE: Newspaper clipping of Ronnie Sr.,
the "Big Cabin dog handler," who swept the
West with three of six dog-trial wins

RIGHT: Ronnie Smith,
Sr., with Storm Victor

Dogs in training with Ronnie Smith, Sr.

Eastern Oklahoma and nationally. The respect for these men and their ability with dogs made a lasting impression on the Smith boys; Dad and Delmar determined early on that they wanted nothing more than to spend a life training horses and bird dogs, and they set a course by that star. It proved to be a course that they, and the rest of the family, would not steer far away from.

By the time Uncle Delmar was in his early 20s, he'd already spent his youth working for mentors John "Skilly" Skillman and Dutch Epperson (who would later become his father-in-law). Newly married, Delmar and his young wife, Jeanne, moved to Edmond, Oklahoma, to take over Dutch's kennel and to begin working dogs for Delmar's own group of clients. Not long after, Delmar achieved some notoriety on the field-trial circuit, where his ability as a trainer was recognized with a series of placements. At that time, Delmar worked many different pointing breeds, but he was fortunate early on to have some very good American Brittanys in his trial string, and this at a time when the breed was becoming more and more popular in the US. When the American Brittany Club ran its first National Championship at Carbondale, Illinois, in 1957, Delmar Smith was the handler behind the winner, FC Towsey, a dog owned by Thomas Black. The Delmar/Towsey duo had a repeat win in 1959, and the following year saw Towsey nudged out of the winnings by another dog in Delmar's string, Hol-iday Britt, owned by TJ Cahill. Between 1963 and 1979 there were 13 US Open Brittany Championships that listed a Smith dog as either champion or runner-up. Of the National All-Age Championships run between 1957 and 1978 there were seven champions handled by Smiths. It was largely these wins that helped Delmar begin a family legacy in the Brittany field trials and eventually helped him earn an induction in to the Brittany Hall of Fame. The bloodline of Smith Brittanys remains in high demand today, among both trialing and hunting owners. Smith Brittanys are still represented in our working string and many of them still go back to the old Towsey and Holiday Britt bloodlines.

As Delmar's recognition grew, so did that of my dad, Ronnie Sr., who had remained on the family property in Big Cabin where I grew up. Dad achieved his own successes in training and trialing, and the Smith name became a common one in national bird-dog circles. Through the 1960s and 1970s, generations of pointing dogs moved through the hands of Uncle Delmar and my dad—and later through the hands of me and my cousins. As a family, we all watched each other carefully, experimenting and sharing the results of our work with one another. All the while, we competed against each other both officially and in that familial way that brothers, fathers, sons and cousins do. I guess it was this combination of competitive spirit and kinship that pushed us all to refine and share our training techniques in pursuit of excellence.

In keeping with the traditions begun by Dad and Uncle Delmar, we Smith boys developed a knack for taking "problem" dogs that were gun-shy, man-shy, or otherwise unable to live up to their breeding and getting them to work. Back when Delmar and Dad started, the training methods were crude at best, but dogs were plentiful. Washouts were expected as a standard part of the deal. Building upon what we'd learned from generations of horses, ranch dogs, pointing dogs, and half-domesticated wild critters, our family developed a method of interpreting behavior and working with animals' natural instincts. With time, we put together a training philosophy that was based on working with a dog's natural abilities, development of cues, repetition, and building association. We put together a training program in which a pointing dog naturally came to understand that physical cues have specific meanings.

As years passed, the next generation of Smith trainers, which included me and my cousins, Tom and Rick, joined in the world of pointing dogs in a formal way. As we came to put dogs through a training philosophy that was essentially the same as the one that Dad and Uncle Delmar had been using for years, we added our individual touches to the process. Of course, this method continues to grow and change as we continue to learn and grow. That said, the basic training techniques that we use have been distilled as the sample size of dogs moving through The Smith Training Method has gotten bigger and

bigger. Through all the years that we have been doing this work, generations of Smith bird-dog trainers have learned from the dogs that we were teaching, and we have continued to do our best in seeking help from each other to build upon everyone's experiences.

My dad, Ronnie Sr., began professionally training bird dogs in 1956. A few years after that, he designed and built a kennel on the western portion of the Smith homestead in Craig County, Oklahoma. Dad continued to train and trial dogs for private clients, while also training some of Delmar's field-trial prospects when time permitted. In 1979, Uncle Delmar began running South Texas guiding operations through contacts he'd made with owners in that region. He called upon his boys, Rick and Tom, as well as me and my dad, Ronnie Sr., to help guide in the South Texas quail camps, which rapidly grew to rely on a great number of dogs. At that time, the quail numbers in South Texas were incredible, and the hunting camps were in high demand. In response, upwards of one hundred dogs were required at a single camp to make it through a winter season.

We all suffered a devastating blow in 1982 when my dad was diagnosed with an advanced case of colon cancer. He passed away just a few short months after learning that he was sick, leaving a huge void in our family and in the greater bird-dog community, which had lost one of their best. When my dad died, I made the decision to leave college and return to the

homestead in Big Cabin to take over my dad's kennel and business. Without much time to look down the road, I immediately took up where Dad had left off. I suppose that I know now that my dad and Uncle Delmar had helped lay a strong foundation for my success over the course of their careers, but I also knew at heart that, like my father and uncle, I just loved running bird dogs and watching them develop. Bird-dog training was all I'd ever really known. I had literally grown up in the shadow of legends, watching my father and uncle and cousins as they trained, handled, and trialed the best pointing dogs in the world.

Growing up as I did, I was well aware of animal behavior from the get-go. Day in and day out, throughout my early childhood, I fed and cleaned kennels and watched my dad and uncle train. I studied a kennel-full of dogs every day, and I learned to notice how the dogs communicated and how they responded to both positive environments and stressors. In keeping with tradition, my father had given me, even as a boy, a growing string of client dogs to work through a training program on my own, and he allowed me to present "finished" dogs to paying clients who were often a little bit skeptical of the boy putting their dog through its paces. Even though I never knew another way, I now know that I was

blessed to have been taught by men who didn't accept the popular thinking of the time. My dad, uncle, and cousins long ago determined that success did not require a trainer to force animals to either give in to the will of the trainer and "break" or wash out. Rather, I was taught that if I was curious and watched a dog, the subtle needs of each individual dog would be made clear. While each dog was a puzzle to be laid out and put together, there was also a basic training outline that would work for each. I suppose that is the beauty of the Smith Training Program; it was developed to be universal, but also flexible enough to fit the needs of each individual dog. This training program has proven itself thousands of times over.

Somewhere in the 1970s, just prior to my full-time entry into the training profession, Uncle Delmar took his system of bird-dog training and brought it to the public in a new and pretty distinctive way. Delmar's training seminars were unique among trainers at the time. His techniques were different, largely informed by his ranch experience as a youth, and he wanted to help bird dog owners and handlers by making his system available to them. Through the late '60s and '70s, he'd begun to notice that there were some things left wanting in professionally trained dogs after they returned to hunting homes. Specifically, Delmar and

ABOVE: Quail hunting in West Texas, early 2000s. From left; President George H.W. Bush, middle Rick Smith, right Ronnie Smith; back left Mike Gibson, back right John Marion. OPPOSITE: Left: Ronnie Smith, Right: Rick Smith, Standing: Delmar Smith

Dad realized that even though they could train a dog and present it back to an owner in condition to perform at its best, the training they'd put into a dog had a tendency to become muddied due to a broken line of communication between owner and dog. Delmar regularly saw clients bringing dogs back to the Edmond kennel, not in order to take the dog's training forward, but to have the dog reaffirm cues that had lost their clarity in the dog's mind. A firm believer that the success of the training required investment on the part of both the dog and the owner, Delmar shifted his focus from just delivering finished dogs to helping dog owners understand how their dog was trained and how to effectively handle their dog in order to utilize that training.

The Smiths have always enjoyed working with people, and this approach of teaching people about training has come to be a defining principle of the Smith family's training philosophy. Working up from the foundation that Uncle Delmar laid, my cousin Rick and I were able to take bird-dog training beyond our kennel and give it to a wider public. As a young man, I continued to train and handle pointing dogs, but Rick and I also began to schedule and present seminars across the country, educating would-be dog trainers in the family's methods. Like Uncle Delmar, I came to believe that the process of training a pointing dog alone only established a baseline—I now know that the real art of training requires that the handler understands the training that has been put in place and how to implement the training so it remains strong as the dog encounters a lifetime of new experiences. In approaching dog training with an eye on both ends of the check cord, I have been lucky to fine-tune my awareness of both dogs and people. I continue to learn each day.

Over the past four decades, I have maintained a busy schedule of training, guiding, and teaching that

carries me away from the training fields at home for much of the year. In South Texas during the early 2000s, a bird dog led me to cross paths with a young lady named Susanna Love. Susanna had sent me a rather outlaw-ish German shorthaired pointer to train while she was working on a cattle operation in Australia. She picked up her dog from me while I was guiding hunts in South Texas, and somehow that dog's training never ceased. We have been guiding and training dogs together ever since, and Susanna has become both my wife and my training partner.

Susanna was raised on Persimmon Gap Ranch, her family's cattle operation 35 miles from the small West Texas town of Marathon. She grew up much like me, surrounded by animals both wild and domesticated, whose behavior fascinated her. In addition to the cattle, Susanna and her family all enjoyed exploring the world of dogs, from bird dogs and lion hounds to cow dogs and heelers. Susanna remained very focused on the cattle operation and how to better handle and train animals in general. I guess that we were cut from the same cloth, as we shared a fascination for animal behavior that made for an easy understanding of one another and mutual respect.

We were married on the bank of a river in 2006 during some time off between out-of-state seminars. Susanna left a career as an attorney to take on a significant role in all aspects of our kennel and training program. In 2013, we were blessed with the arrival of our twins, Reagan and Gage. They now join us in our journey, training dogs across the country.

It is always nice to have a partner when taking the long view and setting goals, and when Susanna and I were married, we focused our efforts on defining and refining a training program that could not only be used directly in the training of client dogs, but one that could also be shared with dog owners

Susanna Love

TOP LEFT: Champion Sports Page on point. CENTER LEFT: Ronnie Smith, Sr., with Storm Victor (First Place winner in Open Derby Classic of the Arizona Shooting Dog Championship), Tom Smith with Prejepa's I'm Meg (Second Place winner), and Bob Soden with Fonego Master Charge (Third Place winner). CENTER: Winners of the Eddie Gardner Memorial Shooting Dog Classic, *Vinita Daily Journal*, Wednesday, Oct 8, 1975. ABOVE: Rick Smith and his son Craig present National Brittany Champion Senator T.J., circa 1976.

and trainers across the globe. We therefore expanded the training seminars that I had developed with my cousin, Rick, to help owners and handlers learn our methods in a hands-on learning environment. In the spirit of training the professional trainer, Susanna and I also built out an apprenticeship program that enables professional trainers and dedicated bird-dog owners to achieve certification in Foundation, Intermediate, and Advanced Level training through a series of 30-day intensive courses.

Today, Susanna and I spend each and every day neck-deep in the world of bird dogs. We both work dogs daily, and we both feed and care for our own hunting string, as well as client dogs. I still guide on the historic King Ranch in South Texas and 6666 Ranch in North Texas with our personal dogs. The training system we have developed, which many know as the Silent Command System or simply The Smith Training Method, represents the culmination of nearly three-quarters of a century and literally thousands of dogs. And with each and every dog and owner, it continues to grow and gather focus. The world changes and so does the world's dogs, and we are constantly reevaluating the needs and wants of the hunters and handlers who own those dogs. In the end, however, Susanna and I have committed our lives to watching and learning from the dogs that fill our kennel. With each dog, we continue to learn, and we also feel joy in offering what we've learned to folks who want to enjoy a bird dog doing what it most desires to do: hunt birds. 🐕

Ronnie Smith, Jr.
Osage County, Oklahoma, 2018

1

DEVELOPMENT

There are numerous ways in which a trainer can get a bird dog to achieve certain behaviors. Historically, and indeed today, trainers have put a range of innovative methods to use in reaching the concrete goal of developing a dog that will find and point game birds so that hunters can effectively approach and shoot them. In that way, trainers all share a common goal.

Where The Smith Method of Training differentiates itself is in a holistic approach that takes into account three primary considerations: the psychology of the bird dog, the psychology of the trainer, and a long-standing history of trial and error that results in the most effective and efficient coordination of each. This philosophical underpinning of our method assumes that a well-bred bird dog is something like a beautiful, malleable lump of clay. The raw material exists in that wiggling mass of tissue and bone and genetics, and given skilled direction, that material can become something quite special.

In each trainer who sets out with the intention of creating a great bird dog, a similar potential exists. In embarking on the journey of training a bird dog, though, that trainer must become malleable too, open to working in concert with what the dog is communicating. This process requires careful analysis and self-assessment of the dog and the trainer herself, in order that each teaching opportunity becomes a learning opportunity as well. We are continually grateful for the opportunity to learn alongside our dogs and to become better trainers on their behalf. Becoming a trainer is a process that has no end.

Daily we see this relationship evolve. We at Ronnie Smith Kennels feel strongly about our methods because we continue to refine them. Each day, we make subtle adjustments that impact our philosophy and our practice. In turn, we continually see our dogs becoming a bit better. That is not to say that in the thousands of dogs we have worked with, each one performs a bit better in the field; such a claim would be unfair and untrue. What we see, however, is that with each dog that we leave our fingerprints on, we are afforded greater insight into what works well and what does not. Through that process, we improve and we feel our dogs do too.

In this section of the book, we explore these philosophies and the methods we employ to activate them. We look hard at what is required of dogs and trainers to achieve that malleable, energized, nimble, and eager-to-learn mindset that makes for a great training experience. This section delineates what is required in the first stages of training a bird dog, and it addresses the processes that often take place before we as trainers ever put our hands on a dog or a check cord.

THE DEVELOPMENT OF A TRAINING METHOD

The Smith Method of Training represents the culmination of years of careful observation and thousands of dogs. It is unique in that it stemmed from a legacy of trainers who were fascinated as much by process as by outcome, and as much by dogs as by the people working them.

Back in the 1950s when brothers Delmar and Ronnie Sr. were getting some notoriety for their success with hunting and trial dogs, the most common approach to bird-dog training was fairly oppositional. In general, people approached animals with the mindset that a desired outcome, a set of behaviors, had to be forced upon that animal. It was assumed that the animal—whether it be a horse, dog, or other creature—would resist this training, and the trainer would either "break" the animal of its undesirable behaviors or the animal would wash out and be considered untrainable. As a result of this mentality, many, many bird dogs suffered fates that they did not deserve, or at least many dogs never achieved the full potential of their breeding. Those that succeeded often did so because their God-given drive and their resilient nature enabled them to withstand a pretty harsh education.

It's worth remembering, however, that the world was a fairly different place in the 1950s. Back then, a fellow on horseback could drift out the back of Delmar's Edmond, Oklahoma, kennels and follow a brace of dogs for miles without crossing a paved road. Handlers and scouts like Ronnie Smith, Sr., could trace the field-trial route along Big Cabin Creek on horseback with the promise of prairie chickens and wild quail in number. Back then, bird dogs were certainly a valuable part of a country lifestyle, but they were seen less as pets and more as tools in a sportsman's tool kit, much like a gun or a saddle. There were dogs that were both loved and appreciated, as well as dogs whose names remain legendary in some circles, but it was also assumed that some dogs would not train, some would run off and be lost, and some would fall victim to the accidents or illnesses that were, and to a lesser extent remain, perils for all working animals. Attrition was part of the program, to the point that many bird-dog trainers never even started working a dog until its first year had passed, at which point any evidence of physical deformity or disability had revealed itself, and the pup had survived the vulnerabilities of distemper and other diseases likely to strike in the first year. Failure was expected, both physically and in training, and this shaped much of the teaching philosophy of the handlers. Dogs either made their way through the fine mesh of the process or they didn't.

Delmar and Ronnie Smith, Sr., differentiated themselves from the popular wisdom largely on account of their childhood experiments "contesting" horses and coyotes and the gun-shy, man-shy, or otherwise unserviceable dogs from other trainers. The practice of carefully watching an animal and shaping its behavior through exercises of repetition, association, and point of contact instilled in them a belief that nearly any dog could learn to handle in the field. Delmar and Ronnie Sr. had a knack for fixing those washed-out dogs—through a life watching

With time, the Smiths arrived at a training program that enabled them to draw the best out of a dog while leaving the spirit of both dog and trainer intact. Thus began a complete stair-step progression that has been continually modified and improved since the '50s, informing the seminars that Delmar started in the '70s, as well as the training that Rick and Ronnie taught to countless owners and trainers through the '90s and 2000s. This method, which we will refer to in this book as The Smith Training Method, or alternatively the Silent Command System (SCS), enabled hundreds of Smith dogs to win field trials, to make bird-dog history, and to be successful hunters across the country. The Smith Training Method resulted in countless satisfied dog owners and even more wonderful days afield for dogs and owners. This philosophy is the backbone of what is put to effective use in the work Ronnie Smith and Susanna Love do today, and it is also the underlying concept behind the training methodology in this book.

Anyone who has seen Ronnie Smith and Susanna Love at work will attest that they are driven by the conviction that anything worth doing is worth doing well, worth doing with purpose, and worth doing with care.

animals, they had proven a system for working those "unfixable" problems out. The elder Smiths operated on a principle that dogs were bred to follow their instincts and could be taught to accomplish those intended behaviors to a high level of proficiency by an observant handler. When dogs didn't perform as they were bred and taught—if they failed to handle, point, or hold steady—the Smiths simply believed that there was a roadblock in the dog's process of understanding the desired outcome. Delmar and Ronnie Sr.'s ability to refine those behaviors and to solve the unfixable problems came from an organic curiosity about a dog's mind. Animal mindset was the interesting part, and the elder Smiths spent an early career setting up environments that would shine a light on unwanted behaviors in order that they, and their dogs, could work through them.

But all of this family history, provenance, and proven success aside, there remains the basic question motivating the chapters to come: *Why?* Anyone who has seen Ronnie Smith and Susanna Love at work will attest that they are driven by the conviction that anything worth doing is worth doing well, worth doing with purpose, and worth doing with care. But in setting out to write a book about training a bird dog via The Smith Training Method, wading back through three-quarters of a century of history, two generations of Smith trainers, and literally thousands of dogs—it is worthwhile to start with this most basic question.

So *why* teach a dog to handle, to do our bidding, to find and point birds? *Why* spend the time and energy to learn to train a bird dog when there are folks across the country, Ronnie and Susanna

included, who are paid to do so professionally? And *why* use the methods illustrated here versus any of the other methodologies out there? As with all good questions, there are a few good answers.

Formal training provides the same foundation for a dog that a formal education provides for a child. It gives the dog a broader base of knowledge to draw from in life. The main goal in training a dog or teaching a child is to develop a confident, well-rounded individual who can think on his own and make good decisions based on his experiences. By training a dog, we help him reach his full mental potential and help him become an animal that has a good life and is a pleasure to be around, both in the field and at home.

The Smith Training Method is a complete step-by-step training system that incrementally builds behavior. It follows a progression that begins with a puppy and finishes with a mannerly bird dog that is the best he or she can be in the field. The system focuses on bringing out natural ability; teaching cues to modify behavior, such as teaching dogs to

heel or be steady on game; and teaching owners how to utilize the training to maintain proficiency in both the home and field.

Philosophically, The Smith Training Method offers the dog and the trainer the opportunity to build a working relationship based on mutual respect, understanding, and points of contact. Approaching the training process with the mindset illustrated throughout The Smith Training Method forces a handler to watch and learn from the dog, see its behaviors and responses, and encourage the preferred outcomes. It creates a smooth and efficient process of training, resulting in a dog that is a good canine citizen and effective in both field and home. The Smith Training Method, when followed properly, ensures success for both the dog and the trainer, enabling the trainer to steer his or her dog and to celebrate the progression of learned behaviors that result in a dog that can find birds, point birds, and remain steady as those birds are either flushed or shot. It also facilitates the opportunity to teach a trainer to fully appreciate, understand, and communicate with a dog that has been bred for centuries to be exceptional at a specific task—therefore affording the trainer a more intimate knowledge of and deepened respect for the bird dog's genetic ability.

There is also a contextual reason for this training. Increasingly, there is a need for people to teach their own dogs because an understanding of the dog's training helps ensure success. As noted above, the greatest breakdown in professional training occurs when the dog returns to the owner, and the lessons learned are not maintained. Whether the following training guidelines take an owner from start to finish or simply maintain the lessons that have been implemented, the more empowered the owner is by a replicable, stair-step progression, the more successful they will be. Central to that training is our personal belief that people must learn to understand the animal that they live and work with. A history of training bird dogs has illuminated that there is some degree of disconnect, perhaps an increasing degree, with that concept. This book is geared to help educate owners about their animals and about the ways that they effectively—and ineffectively—

A dog with a trained mind is a well-rounded animal and will invariably get more opportunities to experience the world and hunting environments than a dog that is poorly socialized and untrained.

interface with those animals. The lessons that follow come as much from a lifetime of training dogs as from watching people training dogs and achieving success through a genuine and *learned* awareness of what the dogs are communicating. In general, the greatest degree of responsibility for the dog's success relies on the owner's ability to observe and understand the dog itself.

This book and this method are also necessary with respect to the times that we live in. No longer can a fellow on horseback trip out the back of Del-mar's Edmond kennel and follow a dog for miles in hopes of finding wild birds. Today, in Edmond, Oklahoma, as in much of the country, the majority of people live in urban or suburban environments, and they don't have the time, the space, or the experience of a lifetime of bird dogs required to be successful. Time has become the great nonrenewable resource in an increasingly busy culture, and that has demanded of Ronnie and Susanna a training format that can be tailored to fit any dog, while remaining efficient in its execution. The process of training a young dog to handle in a streamlined method to the point that he understands precisely what is expected of him in the field is a time-consuming endeavor, so having a proven method is a big time-saver. Time is precious; in this day and age, we need to be increasingly thoughtful and proactive about maximizing the time we do have both for training and hunting our dogs. A proven progression, such as The Smith Training Method, acknowledges that the years of a bird dog's life and the moments to hunt that dog are all too few—they should be fulfilling, not frustrating.

A properly trained dog is a better citizen in the home, in the car, and at the vet. A dog with a trained mind is a well-rounded animal and will invariably get more opportunities to experience the world and hunting environments than a dog that is poorly socialized and untrained. With bird-dog ownership—and all dog ownership—comes the requirement of upholding the owner's end of the bargain. Time and again, owners arrive at Ronnie Smith Kennels at wits' end, frustrated with a dog that is out of control. In our experience, it is not uncommon at the end of the training for an owner to be reduced to tears when he or she becomes able at last to be in control of a dog.

This method works because it is progressive and linear without being rigid. With the concept of understanding behavior and mindset as the backbone, The Smith Training Method provides a replicable platform to implement and maintain an education. The more the owner knows about the training format and how it relies upon an understanding of animal behavior, the more successful

the dogs will be in the training field, the hunting field, and the home. The actual Smith Method of Training is simply a series of exercises that serves as a reference point or template for people to take a dog from start to finish, building upon lessons learned and allowing for an easy step back in the progression when roadblocks are encountered. It is, once again, a stair-step method of training and maintaining.

From the standpoint of a hunter or handler's aesthetic, this system further enhances the experience in the field. There is good reason for The Smith Training Method to have also been termed the Silent Command System. In developing a training methodology based on conditioned response, point of contact, prey drive that outpaces the stress of the learning process, and a minimum of verbal commands—the hunting field becomes a much more relaxing place. A hunt that is filled with shouted commands and whistle blasts can quickly become confusing, turning what should be fun into a tense and disruptive experience. Moreover, when the hunting field is filled with shouts and whistles, the potential for things to go wrong is heightened, and safety can be impacted. With the method outlined in the coming chapters, even the training process is quiet, composed, and fairly relaxed. In fact, the calm, quiet confidence of the trainer is a prerequisite, and it tends to take the dog from a tense or anxious mindset to a softer, more understanding one in which expectations are clear and behavior is not a matter of question.

Fundamentally, though, the answer to the question of *why* is the same answer that has kept two generations of Smiths—and countless generations of bird hunters and dog trainers—engaged in this game. The answer grew out of whatever motivated people long, long ago to select and breed for a dog that had a knack for sniffing out something of value in the tall grass and scrub and to telegraph that presence by means of a suspended instinct to chase. Over the centuries, hunters came to see that watching a bird dog in action was to see pure athleticism at work, independent of the promise of a piece of meat. Those hunters saw a dog on point

as the ultimate expression of suspended animation and the ultimate embodiment of suspense; somewhere up the scent cone was the very thing that both hunter and bird dog had been looking for but could not necessarily see, and somewhere in the coming moments, it would become real and take flight. Whatever relationship between dog and hunter that initially served only to fill the game bag began to stir something deeper in the hearts of people like Ronnie Smith and Susanna Love. For folks like them and the folks reading this book, it is clear that a magnificent animal that is bred for a specific job should be enabled to do that job to the very best of its ability. People who respect animals—those who are amazed by the athleticism, and possibly the magic, that a bird dog embodies every time it locks on point—feel a degree of obligation to make the most of those traits. It becomes a responsibility.

Reid Bryant

THE RELATIONSHIP BETWEEN DOGS AND THEIR TRAINERS

No successful training methodology fails to address the intricate relationship between dog and trainer. Often, training is seen as unilateral, meaning that the trainer puts action upon a dog to achieve a result. The Smith Method of Training is much more democratic; here we explore how a dog and a trainer must work together to achieve mutually beneficial goals.

In order to successfully train a dog, a trainer must first develop a basic understanding of and respect for a dog's true nature. The Smith Training Method hinges upon the ability of a trainer to communicate intended behaviors and to interpret the messages a dog sends throughout that learning process. Clear communication and consistency build behavior—bird dogs and their handlers make up a cohesive team in the field and each relies on the other in order to be successful. If the dog's handler doesn't have a clear understanding of who the dog is—the dog's mindset and personal nuances—the team will be ineffective. Our goal as trainers is to understand how our personal relationship with dogs affects their mindset and performance, provide an environment where they can flourish, and give consistent cues and routines so they can learn how to reliably make good decisions for a lifetime of hunting.

A wonderful reality about dogs is that they are incapable of deceit, and they will always show you their state of mind by means of body language and actions. They will never pretend to understand a situation or a lesson if they don't, which in many ways makes the job of training and handling much easier. The challenge for most handlers lies in learning how to interpret what it is that the dog is saying—this is a skill that can best be developed by paying close attention to how a dog carries itself, moves, and responds to new situations. Dogs are champions of communicating through body language, both in terms of what they tell us and in their ability to assess what we are telling them with our posture, tone, smell, and even the subtlest facial gestures, intentional or not.

Many owners and trainers rely heavily on spoken language when they set out to communicate with their animals. By all means, animals do learn to interpret some of the words we use through associa-

tion. That said, it is easy to forget that spoken words, in general, do not amount to a significant portion of what the animal absorbs and processes mentally. In many ways, a similar statement could be made for the effectiveness of language between humans. Generally, dogs are credited with being able to understand about the same amount of human language as a toddler. To help you understand their view of our modern world, put yourself in their shoes: Pretend you are in a foreign country where everyone speaks a language of which you have mastered only the very basic terms. In that circumstance, you must quickly learn to assess situations and infer what people might be trying to say through a range of nonverbal cues. What people often forget is that the most effective and universal language to use in communicating with animals is body language. Becoming a student of body language, both your own and that of your dog, will help you communicate with your dog most effectively. This awareness is the bedrock of The Smith Training Method.

THE DANGERS OF ANTHROPOMORPHISM

As you start to look more closely at animal behavior, you will see the complex nonverbal language that your dog has been sharing with you all along. That said, you have to remain aware of your own human tendencies for applying a human filter to animal language. Clearly, some behaviors are easy to read: When a dog raises his hackles and growls, it is easy to see that you are better off not tangling with that animal. That said, most behavioral indicators are not quite so blatant, and they may take some time and dedication to learn, to identify, and to interpret. In our experience, the single most common factor that slows the process of understanding canine communication is a tendency in trainers and owners towards anthropomorphism. Humanizing dogs through anthropomorphism and ignoring their true nature creates a roadblock in communication and works to the detriment of both your dog and your training process.

A dog does not comply with your wishes or act against your wishes for emotional reasons. A dog does not like or dislike a human in the way that a fellow

human likes or dislikes a human, nor does a dog wish to please a human for the same catalog of reasons that a human sets out to please another human. Dogs do not express behaviors based on any sense of obligation to their owner or any desire to get a response from their owner in human terms. Dogs simply do not view the world in the same light that humans do, and fully grasping this concept dictates your ability to effectively communicate with your dog.

So, what exactly is anthropomorphism, and how does it apply to your relationship with your dog? For the sake of this discussion, anthropomorphism describes a human-centered way of interacting with the world by giving human characteristics to non-human entities. Anthropomorphism occurs when you take your personal human experiences and interactions with other humans and use them to interpret animal behavior. Dogs, in particular, are regularly subjected to this treatment because they live in our homes with us, they sleep in our beds, and, at times, they even eat our food. Humans generally feel a very close kinship with dogs, whom we long ago gave the title of "man's best friend." With such closeness, it is no surprise that humans tend to interpret a dog's behaviors as we would those of a fellow human. The majority of people who care for animals are guilty in some way of anthropomorphism. The kicker, and the secret to being efficient and effective as a trainer, is to learn to recognize this tendency in ourselves and keep our feelings in perspective. We absolutely must observe and respect dogs for their God-given canine nature in order to be successful in training and helping them in life.

In a complex way, our culture teaches us at a very young age to accept anthropomorphism. We readily accept the idea of Mickey Mouse, a talking rodent dressed in red trousers and white gloves who stands on two feet. Donald Duck, in his blue sailor shirt and cap, is admittedly a little more difficult to understand when he speaks, but he is equally lovable. Children's books and movies as a genre leverage a broad and intricate cast of great anthropomorphic animal characters who teach children to interpret animals through a human lens. Sadly, this use of anthropomorphism seems to lead us down a road of misunderstanding our natural world that in turn hampers our ability to see it in its true radiance.

It would be indisputably wrong to say that animals don't have feelings or emotions; they clearly do. Anyone that has seen a dog excited at his owner's return to the home can attest to that. Dogs particularly have a rich social life; they have emotional attachments, and they are acutely able to read body language and react to it. We know irrefutably that dogs have feelings and personalities; however, to label their actions with our emotions and feelings sets them up for failure.

Anthropomorphism does not allow us to see our canine friends as they truly are. When we project human rules onto dogs, their needs are not adequately met and they are not fully respected for their abilities. This unfortunate trend leaves owners ill-equipped to identify canine behaviors and unable to help their animals be wholesome canines.

To treat your dog as you would a child can reinforce a negative or fearful state of mind. To reward, pat, or cuddle your dog when he is in a fearful or anxious state of mind reinforces that uneasiness and does not have the intended calming effect. Dogs do not understand our meaning when we say, "Baby, it is okay. That trash truck comes every Wednesday. It's not going to hurt you. It is just a big, old, loud piece of machinery—nothing to worry about." Instead, what they know with certainty is that the big truck was alarming enough that it caused you to change your normal calm demeanor and that you went out of your way to coddle them and reward them for running and hiding. Simply telling your dog that the trash truck is not going to hurt him implies to the dog that you too are concerned enough about that trash truck to note and affirm his misgivings toward it. In the dog's lexicon, your attention and response indicate that you too believe that he is doing a good job being afraid and that fear is the logical and intended correct response.

In seeing their world through an anthropomorphic lens, you create more problems than you solve. Talking to your dog generally does not give him the tools he needs to deal with new or stressful situations. As you gain an understanding of animal behavior, it may be helpful to acknowledge that the majority of what humans say to animals is honestly for human benefit; it makes us feel better. If you are able to remove the veil of anthropomorphism, you will more readily see the world through your dog's eyes. When you incorporate your dog's views and norms into your relationships with him, you will end up treating your dog more fairly and with much more respect. This, in turn, allows you to help your dog learn from experience, therein becoming better equipped to handle challenging situations in a healthy way.

RESPECTING A DOG FOR WHO HE TRULY IS

So, let's approach this conversation with a good look at canine language and how dogs truly communi-

Dogs particularly have a rich social life; they have emotional attachments, and they are acutely able to read body language and react to it.

cate. Mama dogs communicate their authority with clarity and consistency. They use physical touch, most frequently a gentle but firm mouth to the neck to move the pups, steer them, or correct them. From the first days of life, clear boundaries are established as the dam asserts a leadership role. She is both teacher and caregiver, like any good, strong, consistent parent should be. The puppy stage is a whirlwind of experience: Pups gather information rapidly and explore their relationships and environment, determining what behavior is appropriate in specific scenarios. Pups nip at times, try to climb to the physical top of the pile sometimes, and attempt to jockey their way past littermates into optimal feeding positions. Somewhere in this process, pups exercise all of those behaviors embedded in their DNA that help determine individual roles within the society of their pack. Those pups that are strongest, most assertive, or most physically adept may well take on different roles within the group than their less forceful littermates.

When a pup is removed from the litter environment at about eight weeks of age and put into a direct relationship with a human owner, there is the potential for the fast-developing roles within the pack—notably with dam and littermates—to unravel. Most owners receive a single dog that quickly becomes the sole focus of attention. The pup leaves the comfortable routine of the whelping pen and enters the home, where a whole new set of behavioral boundaries are established. Relationships are quickly formed and lasting behaviors are cemented within a short amount of time. It is helpful if relationships, roles, and boundaries are established from the very moment that the pup is received by the owner, and it is also helpful to ensure that the new structure is consistent and fair.

Often, owners assume that a new pup needs extra human assistance during this time of transition into the new home. Owners tend to succumb to a human interpretation of what the puppy may be going through. A pup may be given a free pass to engage in behavior that is seen as fairly insignificant in light of the circumstances. Specifically in the early stages of puppy ownership, owners are often lenient about chewing on household items (and humans), licking, jumping up on people, or barking to be let out of a crate. Puppies are conditioned quickly, and if a routine is set, they will happily follow it.

A lax approach to acceptable behavior is often fine and dandy until the puppy grows a little bit, and the consequences of that behavior begin to have a greater and more noticeable impact on the household. When bad manners become a problem after a standard of leniency is set, it can be difficult to reshape that established behavior. If you do not want the full-grown dog on the couch, don't allow the puppy on the couch. If you do not want the full-grown dog chewing on your fingers, don't allow the puppy to chew on you. If you do not want the full-grown dog jumping on your nice clothes, do not allow the puppy to jump up. If you do not want the full-grown dog sitting in the field, do not teach him to sit as a puppy. Think ahead to what may become issues for your dog once he is grown and change the scenario before the issue is created.

It is beneficial to a dog to know what he can and cannot do at any point in time. This requires that you be consistent in your behavior and clear in the expectations of what you will or will not allow. Clarity makes it easier for a puppy to enjoy a healthy and strong relationship with you. It should be your goal to create an environment that will help you develop a healthy-minded adult animal.

DOGS' RELATIONSHIPS WITH INDIVIDUAL PEOPLE CHANGES THEIR BEHAVIOR

All of the interaction that takes place between a human and a dog builds a distinct relationship that determines how the dog will act around that human. When a trainer is called upon to train someone else's dog, a unique challenge and a unique opportunity can arise. When a dog comes in for training, it often brings along a definite set of behaviors, both desirable and undesirable, that were permitted by the owner. Within a few short training sessions, the trainer is often able to reshape the dog's behaviors within their new relationship with the dog. Interestingly enough, those undesirable behaviors often reappear immediately when the owner steps back into the picture. This demonstrates that boundaries and rules can be set within a dog's individual relationship with each person. For example: It is okay to jump on person A, but is against the relationship rules with person B.

As trainers, our mindset affects how any workout progresses. If we are mad, unhappy, distracted, or generally out of sorts, it will show in our demeanor. Since dogs are very accomplished at reading body language, they are also very in tune with the emotions of the people around them and easily pick up on our state of being. The most productive workouts we personally have with our dogs in training at Ronnie Smith Kennels are those that take place when we are "in the zone." These are times when the outside world has minimally impacted our human mindset and we are able to focus intently on each individual dog, remaining closely in tune with their needs and mental processes. At these times, we find that dogs tend to "join up" and become willing and contented members of a working team. These ideal workouts are the most effective for advancing dogs to new levels of training, bringing dogs out of fearful mindsets, teaching dogs to listen to even the slightest cue, and changing their overall outlook to a more positive, constructive mindset.

The worst possible time for humans to work with animals are times when we are frustrated, tired, or just plain mad about something in our lives. Instead of moving our training progressively forward toward a singular goal, these human emotions can actually cause a dog's training to regress, sliding backwards in confusion or with a new undesirable behavior showing up in the training session. Frustrated or poorly timed cues from a handler can bring unnecessary confusion into a workout. Confusion is a roadblock to learning and costs time in the training format. Once confusion enters the training field, all positive momentum stops until that confusion is addressed.

In order to facilitate an efficient training environment, think through your mindset before ever starting a training session. Are you calm and in a positive state of mind? Do you have a lesson plan and know what you are going to ask of the dog? Do you know what your correction will look like if your dog makes an infraction? Do you have a goal in mind to accomplish with your workout? If you can enter a training session with calmness, focus, and the conviction that you are the leader and teacher, progress is more likely to be smooth and you are more likely to facilitate the development of a healthy-minded animal. If you feel yourself getting frustrated, are unsure of how to respond to a dog's behavior, or find yourself distracted from your training by other things in your life, back away and clear your mind. A good trainer has an instinctive understanding of when their state of mind is negatively impacting a workout. In cultivating a calm and confident mindset in ourselves, we can cultivate a confident, engaged mindset in our dogs.

The most effective trainers often show a relaxed demeanor with an authoritative, yet kind, voice and they quietly require the same behaviors from their dogs every day. When they give a command, they quickly make sure that it is followed, and then they move forward to the next activity.

To be an effective dog trainer, act as a leader that you would like to follow, a leader whose team you would like to be a part of. Always keep the team's long-term goals in mind and work toward them in a dedicated manner. Be concise and convey purpose and direction to your teammate. Be fair, be honest, be calm, and be that person that is strong enough to rely on. Don't be the person who lets the petty things ruffle any feathers, and don't sit back to see what happens. Take control and keep your teammate successful.

Every moment with a dog is a teachable one, and we should recognize that there is no interaction with a dog that doesn't shape how it views and reacts to us. Every time that we touch a dog, we shape it—either to the dog's benefit or detriment. We leave our fingerprints on a dog every time we touch him, and as professional trainers, we are hypersensitive to that fact and strive to make sure every interaction that a dog has with us is a positive, healthy experience. 🐾

RAW MATERIAL: PICKING A PUPPY

At Ronnie Smith Kennels, we understand that picking a puppy can be an emotional process and a critical one. It can also be quite enjoyable. Puppies are the raw material with which we embark on a lifetime of learning. Here, we explore how to best ensure that thoughtful choices throughout this process result in a positive long-term experience of owning and working a bird dog.

The adventure begins with picking a good bird-dog prospect. This is always an exciting stage, because unlimited potential and opportunity exist in every pup. As you consider a pup, you can—and should—envision that well-trained dog traversing the countryside in the pursuit of game. You should imagine him proficiently locating game and then intensely standing steady until a hunter approaches to flush the birds—this is the stuff that dreams are made of. Hunting over an upland dog offers the same overwhelming rush of emotion, whether the backdrop is the grouse woods of Minnesota, the prairies of Eastern Montana, the palmettos of Florida, or the mesquite scrub of Texas. An exquisite, focused bird dog on point in the field is what you are working toward, but first, you must pick the right pup to make your dreams a reality.

CONSIDER THE OUTCOME

Buying a bird-dog puppy is unique in that you are buying a playful, eight-week-old bundle of potential and hoping that in a year or two, it will turn in to the dog of your dreams. In that way, picking a pup is a gamble. Certainly, it is a process that requires you to do all sorts of research to hedge your bets, doing everything possible to shape the future for both you and your dog. In the

ABOVE: Picking a puppy is a process that should be approached with excitement and consideration. Be honest about your needs and wants, and let the fun begin.

end, however, picking a pup requires you to take a significant leap of faith, and to simply enjoy the process of sculpting a living, breathing creature.

In looking at potential dogs, it is important to remember that a puppy represents a big investment of time, money, and care. Nonetheless, in every puppy there is the potential for years of precious shared moments and memories that will last a lifetime. So, as you set out to find your perfect bird dog, be honest in your assessment of both the dog you intend to bring home and your own expectations for that dog. It's also important to recognize that you are not selecting a perfect, factory-built product from a manufacturer. Dogs are like people in that individuals excel in some areas while remaining marvelously flawed in others. That said, given an honest assessment of your individual lifestyle and needs, you may very well find a particular dog that is a perfect match for your stage in life and your style of hunting. A perfect dog is one that fits perfectly into your individual lifestyle and expectations.

But how do you determine what sort of dog fits your lifestyle needs? What are your field requirements for that dog? Answers begin to come after an honest assessment of what constitutes your intended result and an honest look at why you want a bird dog in your life to begin with.

At Ronnie Smith Kennels, we have a specific set of criteria upon which we base our personal puppy selection. The dogs in our string are selected for attributes that help us guide our wild-bird hunts in specific locations. We personally like a dog that goes to the country and runs a big race. We guide in tough country and have to cover many miles on a regular basis on our hunts. We need tough dogs with a lot of endurance and stamina to match the landscape and cover. We affectionately say these dogs have more heart than sense, because they keep pushing to find birds when other dogs might quit due to the demands of the environment.

We need dogs that are level-headed and whose "marbles roll right," meaning they are able to think on their feet and typically react in a reliable way. This type of disposition makes training a dog easier and really just makes life with that dog much more

enjoyable. In our case, a dog possessing intellect and level-headedness allows us to be more efficient in our training process and allows a dog to fit more rapidly and seamlessly into our training schedule, our life, and our business. In many ways, our dogs are the tools of our trade, though as living creatures they are also our coworkers. We need dogs that will get the job done, that can be relied upon, and that will not cause us undue stress, time, or trouble. We depend on them to put on a good performance in every type of situation and environment. To do so, our dogs have to have a rational way of mentally processing events and not be flighty or skittish.

Our dogs are with us every day, both in a professional capacity and in a family environment. One automatic disqualification for us is a dog that shows any kind of aggression, either toward other dogs or toward people. Fighting is simply not something that we can have in our kennel or around our family. If a line of dogs is known to have aggressive tendencies, we will steer clear of puppies out of that bloodline.

We look for a dog that has correct conformation as they will be less likely to have health issues stemming from the physical stresses associated with an extended season of work. A dog that "moves lightly on his feet" will be likely to have good endurance. A good deep chest generally benefits the lungs and aerobic capacity of a dog, helping ensure an increased level of stamina. Good tight feet, meaning compact feet with toes that are upright and tight-fitting, help to keep undue strain off the ligaments and tendons, thereby keeping a hard-working dog sound in the field. Correct conformation is imperative. We like a dog that moves with a long graceful stride and an economy of motion in the field.

When we set out to look for a pup that meets our personal criteria, we generally look for a breeding that has proven to produce such a dog. What *we* look for in a pup, however, is not a recipe for what *everyone* wants or needs. The dogs that hold a place on our bird-dog string are dogs that other people might get rid of at the first possible opportunity—just because they are ideal bird dogs for our intended use does not mean they will work for every

owner in every scenario. On the flip side, the dog that doesn't make our team is likely the perfect dog for somebody with a different result in mind. To illustrate this point, let us share the tale of a young Brittany we recently sold. She was a dog we had bred and raised, and she had wonderful attributes across the board: She was built remarkably well, had a good nose, proved easy to train, handled her birds very well, and had a wonderful personality. In the end, however, she simply did not run a big enough race for our wild-quail hunts in Texas, and therefore, despite all the positives, she could never make our team. She wound up going to a home in the deep South where she works wonderfully on plantation hunts; she is her new owner's "perfect" dog, and we are glad we found her a role for which she is a perfect fit.

When looking for a puppy, spend some heartfelt time considering what constitutes your "perfect" dog. Think about your pace and schedule, the regions that you will likely be hunting in, and the species of birds you will likely be chasing. If you are hunting prairie birds in big country, you may want a dog that covers a lot of ground. If you are hunting in dense woods, you may want a dog that works a bit closer. If you are going to be hunting preserves and waterfowl, you may want a shorter-ranged dog that excels in retrieving. Determine what your personal requirements are for a dog in the field.

Be honest with yourself about the hunting you will actually do, not the hunting you would like to think you will do. Acknowledge that though we all hope to put in 60 days a season on wild birds in rough country, a rare few can actually do so. If you will be getting out only a few weekends a year, it may not be a good fit for you to purchase a high-energy dog that may be a challenge to handle the rest of the year.

Consider too that a healthy bird dog will give you a decade of service, and that lifestyles and physical abilities can change dramatically over that period of time. Be truthful and confident in your intended use, and then be sure to convey those intentions clearly to the breeders you speak with. Those breeders will be critical players in assessing the raw material that may well produce your perfect bird dog.

PICKING A BREEDER

Picking a breeder is a bit of an adventure unto itself. Over the years, we at Ronnie Smith Kennels have served as breeders and customers in search of both litters *and* breeders, so we have looked at the process of finding and evaluating a breeder from both sides of the fence.

Identifying a reputable breeder is not terrifically difficult, but it does require some study. A good place to start that research is to look for breeder ads in the bird-dog magazines, ask friends whose dogs you like where they got their pups, contact the American Kennel Club (AKC) for a breeder list to reference, or look at the Endorsed Breeder listings on reference pages such as Orvis.com. Better still, attend some field trials, hunt tests, or other bird-dog events in your area, and talk to the owners of those dogs that stand out to you. Perhaps the best place to start is to speak with the owners of dogs you have hunted over, as this reference point provides the most informed insight into the type of dog you might like to wind up with.

Dog folks are generally forthcoming with info about their preferred breeders, as it serves us all to see conscientious breeding and solid bloodlines continue. Look for a breeder with a good reputation who is easy for you to talk to and whose breeding program is aligned with what your needs are. Talk with the breeder about the specifics of their program and what they are looking for in the dogs they breed. Be sure to ask the breeder generally how the sire and dam hunt and what their hunting traits are.

GOOD QUESTIONS TO ASK:

> What are the breeder's expectations of this litter?

> What is the range of each parents in the field?

> What type of birds have the sire and dam hunted and excelled in handling?

> How easy are the parents to work with and how receptive to training were they?

> Do the sire and dam or past litters exhibit a natural retrieve?

> How much handling do the parents generally require in the field?

> What are the parents' dispositions like around other dogs?

> What is the parents' style like on point?

> If house dogs, how are the parents in and around the house?

Breeding bird dogs is a lot of work. It takes dedication. Usually, bird-dog breeders are in the business and the lifestyle for the long haul, and therefore the success of each litter helps promote their line. In many ways, the success of the puppy buyer's experience impacts the success of the breeder directly. Granted, breeders are in the business of selling dogs, but the good breeders know that a dog that is mismatched with a home will cause their business more harm than good, leaving a bad taste in the mouth of both the breeder and the puppy buyer. Good breeders listen and will be honest about steering a potential owner away from a dog or a litter if the match is not a good one. Breeders possess a wealth of information. If you develop a good relationship with a breeder, he or she will usually bend over backwards to ensure your success—and thereby the success of their puppy.

HUNTING APPLICATION AND PEDIGREE

Field-trial titles in a dog's pedigree are a quick way to evaluate a puppy's potential. Each type of field trial has a unique set of parameters in which a dog must excel in order to win. Comparing horseback trials to walking trails is a good example of how different those parameters and required attributes can be. Often horseback trial judges are looking for dogs that cover a lot of country, dogs that are able to

hunt in front of horses that are moving at a fast pace. Walking trial judges, on the other hand, are generally looking for dogs that stay in closer contact with the handler. For this reason, a champion of a walking trial may exhibit a different range in the field than a champion of a horseback trial. As a result of the specific attributes required for excellence in different trial environments, bloodlines have been refined to result in dogs known for performing well in one arena or another. It is a good idea to research exactly what type of championships show up in your dog's pedigree, as a nonspecific field trial champion designation does not actually provide much insight. A bit more specific research will give you a better idea of a pup's genetic potential.

Please don't assume that because a puppy is of national champion bloodlines that it is automatically a good buy for you. One instance that illustrates this point came about when we were contacted by a gentleman who had recently discovered a passion for pheasant hunting on preserves in the Eastern US. As is the case with many who get engulfed in the world of upland hunting, he decided that the time had come for him to elevate the game by buying and working his own bird dog. He did his research and decided that he wanted an English pointer, and a good one. Popular wisdom indicated that the best pups out there should have national championship bloodlines, and thus began the gentleman's quest for the ultimate dog.

This gentleman purchased a very nice puppy sired by the most recent National All-Age Champion bred to a female with multiple wins who also was from an All-Age Champion bloodline. A year or so after buying the pup, the gentleman brought him to us. The dog was about a year old, and the man was at his wits' end. He had wanted to take his new dog on a preserve pheasant hunt that fall but had no confidence that he could do so safely or effectively. The dog had so much run in him and so much drive that the gentleman was sure he would lose him in a heartbeat if he did not constantly handle him to keep him in the small hunting fields at his favorite preserve, extinguishing all hope of a pleasurable hunting experience. Sadly, the gentle-

man was right; the dog he had chosen was indeed a champion-caliber dog, but he was genetically programmed to run big and win horseback trials. The owner had hoped to have a dog that would naturally remain within gun range at all times, going with him through small covers without much handling. Despite the fact that the dog performed true to his genetics and despite the fact that the owner's expectations were not unreasonable, a significant disconnect transpired. Both owner and dog were pushed to compromise their desires and innate abilities to meet in the middle in order to hunt together.

When looking at breeds and bloodlines and individual dogs, look first at the intended application. If you are looking for a close-working pheasant dog, look for a dog whose parents have excelled in that environment. If you plan to field trial, decide what type of field trial you would like to compete in. There are many different styles of field trials and different lines of dogs that excel in different trial environments. Again, your wants and goals must be measured and matched. Look for litters from dogs that have proven themselves in the type of trials that you are interested in. If you plan to have the dog strictly as a hunting companion, look for a dog that does well in the type of hunting environments that appeal to you most.

We always remind people that to pick a puppy is to play in the futures market. There is no guarantee just how a dog will mature. Environmental factors and genetic tendencies will shape each dog, sometimes in ways you cannot easily predict. That being said, your best way to find a pup that suits your needs is always to find a sire and dam that exhibit the traits you hope to see in your own dog and to get a pup out of their breeding.

A NOTE ON BREEDS

At Ronnie Smith Kennels, we often get questions about our preferred breed of bird dog. Often people get a little baffled when they receive the typical response, one that has been delivered a thousand times: "a good one." What many people don't realize is that our answer is honest and heartfelt. There are dogs in nearly all the pointing breeds that work

for us. If you look at our personal hunting string you will generally see Brittanys, English pointers, English setters, and German shorthaired pointers (with a few springers in the mix for special applications). For us, there is no single breed that is best; there are dogs within each breed that excel in different arenas. For that reason, we often encourage owners to settle on the breed that exhibits the most pleasing physical characteristics to them personally. From there, an owner needs to locate the set of parents within that breed that is likely to throw pups with the specific traits he or she is looking for.

Blanket statements regarding breed types are so riddled with exceptions that it makes them wholly untrue. To say that English pointers don't make good house pets makes the majority of the pointers in our kennel an anomaly! There are a wide variety of traits exhibited by individual dogs of every breed.

A NOTE ON GENDER

We have also noticed over the years that there are some strong notions about whether male or female pups make more biddable or driven bird dogs. Certainly, the gender of your pup is worthy of consideration, but it has little impact on the hunting ability of the specific dog. Depending on the breed, there can be some desirable male or female physical characteristics such as size or conformation, but, by and large, these characteristics are also subject to the individual. Some owners just have a preference for males, some for females, and if there is something in your experience that informs that preference, then by all means let it steer your selection.

If you are planning to spay or neuter your animal, we do recommend waiting until at least a year of age. It is our belief that waiting until after the animal has reached physical maturity allows him the benefit of full hormonal balance during his growth.

TO SIMPLIFY

With all of the above considerations in mind, our recommended breed selection process involves some simple, basic steps:

1) First, pick at least one breed whose physical

appearance you like and whose general hunting application fits your needs.

2) Determine the requirements for your particular dog, including what body style and conformation appeal to you personally, what type of personality is a good fit in your home or kennel, and what range and style in the field fits the way you will be hunting or competing.

3) Locate breeders that fit the above criteria and that come with proven references. Discuss with those breeders what specific dogs or line of dogs they think may be a fit for you. Trust the people who are in the business of breeding bird dogs to steer you in the right direction. Referrals and references are a great way to source a breeder that has a litter on the ground in which you may be interested.

4) Trust your instincts, be pragmatic, and be honest with your intended wants and needs. The perfect puppy, or likely several, will be waiting at the end of the process.

NARROWING IT DOWN: PICKING YOUR PARTICULAR PUPPY

Once you have selected a breed and a breeder that you believe will be a good fit for you, the next step will lie in narrowing your choice to just one puppy. Likely there will be some parameters and limitations to your pick based on a variety of factors: You may have pick of the litter, but you may have second pick of females, third pick of males, etc. Within your selection, some breeders may be able to send pictures and video of the litter and of the individual pups from which you can choose. Those resources can provide great background information for expediting the decision-making process and eventually for picking your individual pup. If you decide to pick out of the litter based solely on coloration (Let's face it, by the time you pin down the right breeding, coloration is sometimes the easiest way to differentiate!), pictures help simplify the decision-making process without even seeing the pups in person. It

is critical, however, that you don't rely on snapshots or video clips as hard-and-fast determinants of what a puppy's nature or personality may be. Just because Pup #1 was seen carrying a toy in one picture does not mean he likes to carry things and is therefore going to be a great retriever. Similarly, even if a video of Pup #2 shows him pointing like he could win a national championship, there is no guarantee that this behavior predicts future tendencies. When looking at pictures and videos of individual pups, keep in mind that snapshots and our interpretation of them can skew our perception.

Many great breeders are busy caring for dogs and therefore do not have the ability to inundate you with puppy videos and pictures during the first eight weeks of the puppies' lives. That means that the day you arrive at the breeder's kennel to pick up your puppy may be the first day you see the puppy that is actually going to travel home with you. This can be a challenge, but it is also part of the fun.

On pick-up day, the best guide to selecting the correct puppy for your life will probably be standing right beside you—and no, we are not referring to your three-year-old daughter! The human who knows the individual pups best is the breeder who has been studying the litter, and likely the sire and dam, since the moment they were born. The breeder knows the breeding on an intimate and scientific level; he or she knows which puppy has shown alpha tendencies, which puppy has shown consistently that he likes to carry something in his mouth, which puppy tends to roam by himself, and which puppy runs for cover when something new presents itself.

Let the breeder guide you toward a few puppies that may fit your requirements, personality desires, and lifestyle. After you've arrived at this point in the selection process, either pick the pup that appeals to you most, or close your eyes, reach down into the box, and grab one! The hard work is done, and honestly you will wind up falling in love with any of the pups that meet your generalized criteria.

We often hear people asking Uncle Delmar how he picked so many champion dogs as eight-week-old pups. Delmar is a great storyteller, but he is also a

straight-shooter, and he is absolutely honest when he reveals that often those puppies were the "leftover dogs." He often admits this with a laugh, as he is, in part, still amused at the unpredictable way in which life works out and he is also a little embarrassed that after more than 90 years as a trainer and handler, he still does not have a surefire method for picking out the best puppy in a litter!

Again, picking a puppy is the same as playing the futures market. Once you accept that, the process becomes a lot easier and more fun. You are picking a puppy based on genetics, parental indicators, and the characteristics that a pup exhibits at a tender and rapidly changing age. From there, it is up to you how you mold that little wiggling ball of puppy breath into a focused, bird-seeking companion.

RECOMMENDED CHARACTERISTICS TO LOOK FOR IN A PUPPY:

> **Confidence**: You will want a puppy that exhibits confidence in the company of his littermates. If a pup is skittish in a familiar environment and among familiar dogs, he will likely wrestle with a similar tendency later in life as well.

> **Good overall conformation**: A pup's legs should have correct angulation for movement in the field. He should have tight feet, a balanced body frame, etc.

> **Good overall condition**: The pup should have a shiny, healthy looking coat with a moderate layer of fat over the ribs.

> **Healthy**: The pup should be free of obvious health issues or physical defects.

> **Parasite free**: The pup should have a worming record and an appearance that does not indicate the presence of worms (i.e., poor body score and a large distended belly).

> **Engaged**: The pup should be interested in chasing other puppies, leaves, balls, etc., which is a predictor of prey drive.

> **Vaccinated**: The pup should have proof of current vaccinations.

> **Friendly**: The pup should be friendly and receptive to you.

BREEDER BLAME

It is worth a moment here to remember that breeders are certainly accountable for their service standard, honesty, and business integrity, but they also cannot command the whims of nature. Pups grow and change dramatically over the first few months of life, and if your pup doesn't seem as though he is maturing in quite the way you expect him to or if he develops an unforeseen physical issue, pause for a moment before you call the breeder to ask for compensation. Certainly, obvious physical deformities or anomalies that significantly impact the ability of the dog to work or stay healthy should be addressed with the breeder, but bear in mind that in dealing with animals, we are all dealing with living, imperfect beings. Puppies, like all animals, are the product of a genetic lottery wherein everyone is striving for the best result and managing the variables as well as possible.

A breeder can breed the same pair of dogs for years and get consistent, proven results, and then unaccountably have a litter that is completely different from those produced in all the previous breedings. If breeding dogs was 100 percent predictable, then everyone would have a national championship trophy on their mantelpiece! The more animals you have, the more you will realize that part of animal ownership is the magic and luck of winding up with that one superlative dog that exceeds all expectations.

In buying a pup, you aren't buying a manufactured and guaranteed product off the shelf. To the contrary, you are buying a little bag of genetics and then doing your best to develop potential into the best combination of qualities for your intended use. A breeder can no more foretell the future than you can. 🐕

An understanding of expectations and parameters is a good place to begin any dog-training conversation, and a critical platform from which to welcome your pup into the family.

GETTING THE RIGHT START: PUPPY DEVELOPMENT

Like human children, puppies need to be set up for success. By properly considering how we condition our pups to respond to the big wide world before them, we can maximize the ease with which they achieve their full potential.

Picking a pup puts the wheels in motion for a wonderful ride, and once the wheels are in motion, so are you. Trust the genetics of the pup, trust the potential of the process, and move immediately into the aspects of socialization, mindset, and training that you can control. This process begins immediately as the lessons that are imprinted on a puppy from six weeks to eight months of age will be present for life. Once you have a pup in your possession, there is an awful lot you can do to ensure positive movement along a path towards success.

EXPECTATIONS: WE ALL NEED TO KNOW WHAT'S EXPECTED OF US

Many owners have bird dogs that also live in the home, and as such, there can be some lack of clarity around whether the bird dog is a pet or a working animal. There should be no differentiation in your approach to boundaries and expectations based on where or how your bird dog lives—the end goal is always a healthy-minded animal that is a pleasure to be around and can confidently navigate life.

An understanding of expectations and parameters is a good place to begin any dog training conversation and a critical platform from which to welcome your pup into the family. All of the animals that live in our house are also working bird dogs. We approach them as we would any dog, and we have the same expectations of them whether they are on a hunt or watching a movie with our kids.

Consistency is the key to building replicable behavior in different environments. This consistency is what helps dogs perform at the highest level. We monitor our dogs' behaviors in our home to ensure that their interpretation of boundaries in the house does not confuse or negatively impact their performance in the field. The rules they learn in the kennel apply in our house, whether it be politely waiting their turn at the door or heeling calmly on a loose lead. Asking a dog to be the same animal everywhere he goes will help him become successful and confident. It is not fair to allow a dog to be out of control around the family and then ask him to be a mannerly performer in the field. If manners are enforced in the house, it will be easier to enforce them at a distance in the field.

By definition, consistency requires you to enter a relationship with a puppy based on unchanging expectations for behavior. Remember, from the moment you first lay a hand on your puppy, you are molding the animal that he will become. You are constantly shaping how he views the world and reacts to stimuli.

To help prepare a dog for success in life, you have to be able to communicate with him in a calm, clear, and consistent manner. Start by emulating the behavior you would like your dog to exhibit. If you want a calm dog, be calm around your dog. If you want your dog to stand still when the vet is examining him, use a calm, relaxing touch when you handle him to shape that behavior from day one.

Remember the most common behavior that is allowed with your dog will become his default behavior. That default behavior will show up in times of excitement, stress, or confusion. If you want a dog to be able to stand calmly by your side in the field, don't reward a bouncing puppy with attention until he stands calmly. If you want to develop a good natural retrieve, don't play tug-of-war with your dog as a puppy, as doing so will build in a hard-mouthed default behavior.

DIFFERENTIATION: PETS VS. WORKING DOGS

What is the difference between a pet and a working bird dog, and how does that difference impact the way you raise him?

We often get this question at seminars, and for the longest time neither one of us had a clue how to respond. In our eyes, a bird dog and a pet dog are the same animal with slightly different job descriptions. Regardless of whether a dog's end goal is to find birds or simply be a companion, you must approach the dog in the same way you would approach any other domesticated animal: with love, respect, and boundaries. After fielding this question several times, we realized that we might have misunderstood the assumptions that motivated it. The mystery was finally solved for us when a gentleman in one of our seminars volunteered to shed some light: In that gentleman's words, a bird dog was held accountable for his behavior, whereas a pet dog was allowed to do as he wished and was not provided with a clear set of expectations or rules. With this explanation, the question began to make more sense to us, as did some of the challenges encountered by participants in our seminars. Simply put, in the eyes of many owners, a bird dog abides by rules and expectations and a pet does not. With this perspective, we immediately came to have more empathy for pet dogs and the struggles of owners who are approaching the formal training process for the first time.

RIGHT: Though the dogs in the Smith guide string have a defined job to do, all dogs benefit from a clear sense of purpose. It is the responsibility of the trainer to create boundaries and teach dogs to work within them.

SOCIALIZATION: WHAT IS SOCIALIZATION AND WHY IS IT IMPORTANT?

///

Proper socialization can set your puppy on the path to becoming a healthy-minded individual that interacts well with others and can manage new or stressful situations well. A dog that has undergone proper socialization will be more confident and well-adjusted throughout his life, enabling him to take training with ease and efficiency.

Socialization occurs in stages throughout the pup's early development. Through these stages, the pup likely will move from the mama's immediate care into the care of the owner or trainer. The first substantive period of socialization occurs during the first three weeks of a pup's life. The specifics of canine maternal care evolved over millennia to serve a critical physiological and psychological purpose to support and sustain the species. Maternal presence is critical during this stage, as the pups have limited motor skills. Proper input and physical contact by the dam during this stage helps puppies learn to handle life's stressors, aiding in the development of the pup's nervous system. The mild stress of being handled by humans can assist developing problem-solving skills while also boosting cardiovascular performance and immunity. Puppies that are handled a lot during this age often mature faster and have better cognitive skills as adults than puppies with limited early human interaction.

In addition to positive interaction with people, we incorporate some early neurological stimulation with our puppies within their first few weeks. Research has shown that early neurological stimulation, or the introduction of minor stressors, has benefits for the growing pup, aiding in neurological development, development of the immune system, ability to adapt to new environments, and stress tolerance. Our practice of early physical and neurological stimulation is based on the US military's research and program called the "Bio Sensor" and later the "Super Dog Program." In training dogs for critical military and police applications, researchers and behaviorists found that minor stresses on a puppy during the age of three to 16 days enhanced rapid positive development, allowing puppies to be better suited to dealing with new or challenging situations as an adult. In layman's terms, puppies that undergo a Super Dog Program or a version thereof have better "bounce-back" when dealing with stress.

In essence, the Super Dog Program takes a puppy through five exercises every day from day three through day 16. Tactile stimulation occurs when the puppy is held and the sensitive area between his toes is gently tickled with a Q-tip for three to five seconds. Physical manipulation occurs in the second and third exercises when the pup is held sitting upright for three to five seconds, then held securely upside-down with his head pointed directly downward for three to five seconds, then held supine on its back for three to five seconds. And last, the pup experiences thermal stimulation by being lain on a cool rag—a washcloth that has been placed in the refrigerator for at least five minutes—for three to five seconds. It is recommended that this sequence be done with normal, healthy puppies no more than once a day and only for the short period recommended. Of course, common sense should be exercised if unusual situations occur.

///

We believe this simple process followed by proper socialization helps prepare dogs for various facets and stressors of life, from living in an urban environment to performing on hunts in a range of unfamiliar locations.

The second stage of development in socialization occurs from about four to 16 weeks. From a socialization standpoint, this period is critical as it is often during this time that the pup moves away from its littermates into the owner's home. During this stage, puppies really begin to explore their environment, and they similarly begin to establish and test a set of social skills through interactions with the dam and littermates. During this stage, the dam makes an immense impact on how the puppies view and react to the world. For example, a mama bird dog that is sound-sensitive may startle at any loud noise and run back into the whelping box. In this case, puppies will instinctively cue off the response of their mama and learn that loud noises are cause for alarm. Puppies growing up with a sound-sensitive mother will likely be sound-sensitive as adults. This is one reason that we use whelping pens that have a slam door. At a young age, our puppies learn to associate a loud noise with mama coming in or going out. Our puppies make a positive association with loud noises from day one.

Dogs are pack animals. There are social norms associated with a pack mentality that people cannot teach dogs. Dogs absolutely have to be around other dogs during this second stage of socialization in order to socialize effectively. There are a few things that you can do to help your dog "be a dog" and to facilitate proper and healthy early socialization. First, it is important that you allow a pup to stay with his litter until at least eight weeks of age, provided that the litter represents a safe and healthy environment (exceptions include scenarios in which puppies are being raised by a fearful dam or even an aggressive one). Next, it is key that when the pup comes into your home, you allow him to play with other dogs. Keep an eye on these interactions and make sure they are positive ones; if an older dog is aggressive toward a puppy, he can cause long-term physical or psychological damage to the pup. Older dogs are going to have to "lay down the law" from time to time with a pesky pup, but as an owner, you must make sure that the corrections are justified and not excessive or damaging. Finally, be certain that the pup has an active, dynamic, and stimulating early experience. Expose him to new environments and various canine social groups. Get him out in the world. Despite our busy lives, this period of socialization requires our time, energy, and effort—consider that time spent as an investment in the future that will pay dividends in the aptitude and attitude of the bird dog in your life.

The final stage of socialization essentially follows the dog through its life and enables these early lessons to be cemented. In short, this stage requires that we maintain the learned behaviors and enhance the dog's flexibility and positive response to stressors and stimuli. For practical purposes, this just means that you must keep your dog engaged. Give him new experiences and keep his schedule dynamic. Travel with him to hunt or trial, walk him on a lead through a busy downtown area, introduce him to puppies, older dogs, and a range of people. The greater his exposure through life, the more limber his mind will remain, and the more practiced he will be when encountering challenges in the field and in training.

Note: Poor socialization makes dog more susceptible to all types of stimulation.

FINGERPRINTS

Every single interaction that a dog has with a human leaves a new set of fingerprints on that dog. Uncle Delmar always preached that if you are really in tune with a set of dogs, you can walk through a kennel and pinpoint what member of your training or kennel staff returned each dog to his box or run. The most recent human interaction leaves a unique set of prints on the dog's psychology that impacts how the dog feels, reacts, and responds. Those fingerprints may get covered up with other fingerprints over the course of ensuing interactions, but they remain a lifelong part of who that dog is. Considering this, your fingerprints help make up your puppy's portfolio of behaviors, and that portfolio remains with your

dog for life. Don't let this circumstance intimidate you, but do be aware of it. Think about it whenever you encounter an issue with your dog. We all share responsibility for how a dog acts.

Ideally, every set of fingerprints that you lay on a dog should help to mold his mindset into that of a solid, well-equipped bird dog. In training, the goal is always to impress new and positive fingerprints onto a dog's personality and to attempt to rub out the less desirable fingerprints that have found their way into your dog's life.

PUT INTO PRACTICE: HOW TO PROPERLY SOCIALIZE A DOG

Young dogs need exposure to new things, places, and people. From a socialization standpoint, there are a lot of steps you can take to set a young dog up for success. Expose your dog to the diverse realities of life as much as you safely can. Don't shy away from life's sounds, smells, and unpredictable experiences, and respond to them with calm confidence. When encountering a new situation that stresses your young dog, try to model a neutral demeanor. The reaction that you would like your dog to develop is one of calm acceptance. Try to be that calming influence on him.

Think back to when you have watched a mama dog with her pups. If a pup becomes scared, the mama never follows the pup to its hidey-hole to cuddle him. To the contrary, a mama dog will stand nonchalantly and watch her fearful pup retreat. Reassured that the dam is not concerned about what is going on, the pup will eventually return to stand calmly near her. With repeated exposure to new stimuli, the pup's retreats become less and less frequent, and eventually the pup will stand calmly by the dam's side and cease running away at all. It should be your goal to exercise the same calming influence as a mama dog. Be neutral with your actions and demeanor when something new occurs, especially when your pup seems uncertain. Use your actions—not words—to communicate to your pup that the new event is barely worth reacting to. That type of modeling will give your pup the strength and boldness to face new stimuli or situations with calm and confidence.

Young dogs need exposure to new things, places, and people. Expose your dog to the diverse realities of life as much as you safely can. Don't shy away from life's sounds, smells, and unpredictable experiences.

Unlike in the case of the mama dog, however, it is best not to allow your pup to retreat all the way to his hidey-hole. If he is on a short lead and you simply do not allow him to run off and hide, he will have to face his fear rather quickly and directly, as opposed to going through the full process of deciding to come out of his hidey-hole and incrementally face that fear. With repetition, your pup will get stronger and stronger until he is fully able to encounter new experiences with little to no stress and to deal with new experiences in a calm manner. This will help him mature successfully in all aspects of his life. Of course, use common sense to ensure that your pup is truly and honestly safe and that being held back by a lead will not put him in any kind of danger.

At a young age, dogs are still very susceptible to disease and injury, so exercise some caution regarding where you take your pup. Letting your pup play loose in a dog park with other dogs may not be a good idea because you do not know if there is a dog there that will be aggressive toward him. That said, allowing your pup to play with a friend's good-natured bird dog can impart critical canine social skills to your puppy, benefitting him down the road.

THE EFFECT OF GOOD SOCIALIZATION, EXPOSURE, AND WORKING TO SHAPE BEHAVIOR: SKY'S STORY

At Ronnie Smith Kennels, we are often looking for new lines of dogs to add to our personal hunting string. One spring day we received a call from a gentleman who was looking to sell a couple of pups. The pups were about four months old at the time

When given the right opportunities, many fearful-minded dogs can become bold hunting companions, like Sky.

and therefore substantially older than the dogs we usually like to buy from breeders. That said, the pups were out of a bloodline that we really liked, they were nicely built, and they just had that over-all "look" that we appreciate. The downside to the deal was that the pups had not been properly social-ized. By saying they were not properly socialized, we do not mean that these puppies were neglected. The man who had raised them was very proud of his pups, and he had happily spent time with them every afternoon. The problem was that he was the only human that they ever saw or interacted with, and his daily contact consisted of taking the pups on a walk on the same path through the same field. They grew up on a peaceful farm in a quiet, rural area with a calm, steady, and consistent owner. Theirs was a quiet and invariable routine, and the pups were content and happy in that routine, as long as it never changed.

When we went to look at the pups, five of us arrived at that quiet farm in a strange truck. The

puppies, who were ill-equipped to deal with the newness of strangers on the property, immediately suffered from a stimulation overload. They both ran for cover. It took us the next half hour to slowly coax them out of the trees among which they had hidden. After another few minutes, the breeder was able to catch the pup that we had decided had the most potential for a place in our string. When we put her on a lead to get her to the truck, it looked like we had a bee-stung coyote on the end of a rope! She tried to pull away or lay down at every opportunity, and she fought so hard that she slipped her collar once before we could lead her to the gate. After catching her a second time, we managed to get her to the truck, but Ronnie's toe got caught on the bumper, and he dropped the pup as he stepped up to load her. The frightened puppy ran straight back to the security of her pen, and we began the process all over again.

When we finally got the puppy, whom our kids dubbed Sky, back to our place, she exhibited all the hallmarks of poor socialization. She would run to

the far corner of the kennel to get away from us, she would cower, and she would resist the lead. The first few days that Sky was at our home, she was entirely overwhelmed. Another dog would bark, and she'd jump. Whenever our big blue tractor rolled by her kennel, she could not find a corner dark enough or deep enough to hide in. Every little thing would send her scampering to her crate.

With time, we managed to help Sky face her fears and become accustomed to seeing and interacting with us and with new and unfamiliar stimuli, but the process took time, consistency, and steady reinforcement of expectations. With time, Sky realized that noises and new people were commonplace occurrences that did not necessarily hurt or impact her physically. Through that process, though, her default behaviors remained, and we had to work through and beyond her tendency to run away and hide from stimuli and stressors, such as new people or unfamiliar situations.

The process of socializing Sky simply began by asking her to face stimuli that triggered her flight response. As Sky settled into her new life a bit, we began snapping a check cord to her collar and sitting with her in her kennel. When we would move unexpectedly, Sky would make a dash for her dog box. In response, we would simply stop the rope a few feet shy of the dog box, not allowing Sky to enter the box. Sky would stand there looking at where she wanted to go and thinking about what had frightened her. As she was able to process the situation and realize that the thing that had scared her was not chasing her, she slowly eased her pull on the rope. She began, instead, to turn in curiosity toward the person that had frightened her. In short, she began to face her fears. With repetition and with our commitment to remaining calm, quiet, and neutral in our demeanor, Sky began to realize on her own that the stranger was not something to be afraid of and that she could stand calmly while that person moved around. The process started all over as the we ventured to the new environment outside of the kennel. If an ATV drove by, Sky would make a run toward the safety of her kennel. We would again stand neutral, hold the rope steady,

stop the flight process, and wait. Again, Sky would eventually quit pulling on the rope, think things through, and eventually move toward us and give herself some slack on the rope. This routine taught Sky a multitude of lessons, but most importantly, it taught her to face her fears and to turn off the pressure of a rope by giving herself slack. This was the first "cue" that Sky learned, and it began the process of teaching her to respond to cues, setting her up for success in formal training.

One of the processes that helped Sky the most was simply exposing her to an array of new places and new people. Case in point: Her first trip with us took her well out of her comfort zone, all the way to Mississippi to a seminar we were giving at Gun Dog Supply. We wanted to demonstrate how a dog could be fearful and not be neglected or abused, but rather improperly socialized. We made a side trip to see some friends at a hunting preserve in Mississippi before the seminar, so Sky had the opportunity for a little travel and some experience living on the road. By the time we needed Sky to demonstrate poor socialization at the seminar, she had met enough new people and seen enough new things that she stood proud and confident, gladly letting strangers approach and pet her. She even pointed a pigeon that was planted a few feet in front of the large crowd of seminar participants. She looked like a million bucks! In the end, all that Sky needed to overcome her fears was exposure and stimulation, allowing her to learn that new experiences were not necessarily cause for fear. The trip was a total success for Sky, but a total flop for demonstrating poor socialization!

The moral of Sky's story is that a dog can be cared for and loved, yet remain crippled by not being properly socialized. A dog that is kept in a backyard with a privacy fence and allowed to only interact with its owner is likely to respond to new situations in much the same way that Sky did. Though a dog may be conditioned to its consistent, replicable, and loving environment—he may not be socialized in a way that prepares him for success in the outside world.

Improper socialization and a lack of early and steady exposure to new environments, stimulation, and unfamiliar people can have a long-standing neg-

ative impact. Try to read your dog's behavior correctly and honestly, and help create situations that address his fears, build his confidence, and teach him how to rationally deal with the stresses of life. The caveat to this is a dog that is genetically predisposed to a state of fear. If a dog is fearful—not due to experiences or lack thereof—but due to how he is genetically programmed to respond, he will not be able to rise to the occasion as Sky did. If you see this trait in your dog, analyze it and consider the dog's parents. Were the parents fearful? Could this be a genetic trait that will only respond marginally to socialization? If you conclude that the fearful behavior is likely genetic in nature, it may be time to ask yourself if you want to continue working with this dog and commit to managing this behavior for his lifetime. If so, it will become a part of your daily routine to help him in the same way as we were able to help Sky.

CRATE TRAINING AND HOUSE TRAINING

At some point in your dog's life, he is going to have to be restrained or confined in one way or another. Whether the restraint takes place on a leash in the park, in a crate at the vet's office, or in a kennel during training—a dog needs to learn to be relaxed and comfortable while restrained. Developing this comfort should start as soon as you bring your puppy into the home. Crate-training your pup will help him learn there are times that he can run and get his energy out, and there are times when he simply needs to relax and "hang out."

Start the process of crate-training as soon as your puppy comes into the home. Be sure that you give the puppy a crate that suits his size. If the crate is too large, it will not represent the safe, den-like environment that the pup is used to. Get a crate that is big enough for the pup to lie down in, but not big enough for him to play around a lot. Be prepared to buy a bigger crate as the pup grows. Also, avoid putting blankets, rags, or pillows into the crate with the dog. A simple chew-proof crate pad should be sufficient for comfort and warmth.

If your pup is indoors and not actively playing with somebody or being supervised, that pup needs to be in the crate. When your pup is fresh and ready to play, make sure to take him out for some fun and exercise, typically outdoors. By developing a habit of relaxing in the house and running and playing outside, you will help teach your dog at a young age how to "turn it on" and "turn it off."

It does take a little planning and foresight to efficiently crate-train your pup. First, make sure that he has had plenty of time to run, play, and take care of his physical needs while outside. Ideally, he should have had plenty of exercise and should likely be looking for a comfortable place to nap. When your pup is at this point, place him in his crate. The crate should quickly become his den and a place of comfort for him.

As soon as your pup wakes up, he is likely going to want to pee. Quietly go to his crate, open the crate door, and pick him up. Carry him to a predetermined spot in the backyard. This is going to become his area to pee and poop. Let him down in the grass and walk a little with him. Do not let him back into the house or begin to play with him until he has emptied out. Be consistent with this routine. Keep time in the crate cut into short segments so that the pup can stay successful and never pee in his den. In time, and with consistency on your part, your pup will be successful at always going to the bathroom outdoors and not inside your house or his crate.

The hardest part of crate-training a puppy is not "rescuing" him when he barks or whines. As humans, we have a tendency to think, "My puppy is whining because he is unhappy, and it is my responsibility as his owner to go make him feel better." When you respond to your pup in this manner, you are teaching him to believe that if he makes noise, a human will open the crate. As a result, he will make the logical association that "I get rewarded when I bark and whine." Make an effort to reward the desirable behavior, which is a dog that knows how to be quiet, calm, and patient. If at all possible, do not let your pup out while he is barking. If you can wait until he has been still, calm, and quiet for even five seconds before releasing him, you will be far better off in the long run.

You will help your dog in myriad ways by crate-training him at a young age. First, crate-training helps you start the process of house-training.

Second, crate-training helps your dog become a calm, relaxed animal that everyone wants to be around. Third, crate-training sets your dog up for success in the field by teaching him to rest when he is in a crate and to expend his energy when he is released outside.

Ronnie's cousin, Rick Smith, fondly recalls being at a championship field trial with his string of bird dogs. He had a prospect that was favored to win the national championship that year. The day before the dog was scheduled to run, a friend of Rick's slipped up beside him and quietly suggested that Rick take the dog to the vet. Understandably concerned, Rick immediately asked his friend why. The well-intentioned person reported that earlier in the day, he had walked down the entire line of dogs and Rick's dog was the only one that was not raising a ruckus. The friend reported with some concern that instead of barking and jumping, Rick's dog was laying down calmly and quietly. Upon hearing this report, Rick relaxed considerably and shared with his friend that a calm, reserved demeanor was just that particular dog's way. His was a dog that was able to "turn it off" and "turn it on" like a light switch. He conserved his energy for the "important stuff." That dog did run a championship race the following day and left that field trial as that year's National Champion.

TEACHING YOUR PUP TO LEAD

When you get your pup home, it is entirely likely that he will have never been on a lead before. Your pup's training will start here. When you first put a puppy collar on your new dog, he is likely to start scratching at his neck with his back feet. This response is normal—he is simply scratching at the odd sensation of having something on his neck. With just a little bit of time, he will become accustomed to the sensation of the collar and act normally.

Next, you should introduce the leash, or lead. There are a few ways to introduce the lead to your pup, the most common of which is to simply hold the lead steady in your hand. You can also certainly snap a lead to a pup and let him drag it around, or even tie the lead to a tie-out or stake-out and let the pup sort things out on his own. All methods will work well.

Advanced lead work
with young dog

Advanced lead work
with young dog

If you choose the first approach, holding the lead in your hand provides a great opportunity to start teaching cues without your pup even knowing it. Cueing a dog with a lead will be explained in greater detail in chapters to come, but a cue is essentially a simple tension then a release, indicating that the correct behavior has been demonstrated and rewarded. In introducing these first cues, think of yourself responding to the pup as if you were as stationary and unmoving as a tie-out. If the pup pulls, hold steady, and let the pup create tension in the lead, which creates a cue. When he gives, you give back, reintroducing some slack. This cue and release will teach the pup that the best response to pressure on his collar is to yield to the direction of the pressure. Animals learn on the release of a cue, so make sure to give your pup slack when he moves toward you. Do not take up the slack and keep tension on your pup's collar, as this will teach your dog that there is no behavior that will "turn off" the tension on his collar and therefore no reward in responding to the cue.

If you choose to introduce the lead by allowing your pup to drag a short line around behind him, there are a couple of necessary precautions to take. First, be sure the rope is light enough and short enough that it does not bother the pup or significantly impede his movement. Next, be certain that the rope does not have any knots in it, as knots could potentially catch on obstacles and create a dangerous situation. Finally, it is crucial that you never leave your puppy alone with a lead attached to him. There are just too many things that can go wrong when a pup on a lead is left to his own devices; you as the owner or trainer should be present at all times when your pup is on a lead.

If you choose to tie your pup, just keep an eye on him. Make sure he does not get tangled up in the lead but expect that he will struggle a bit at first, working against the restraint. Once he relaxes and settles down, you can untie him and take him for a walk.

TEACHING YOUR PUP TO BE CALM AROUND PEOPLE AND TO STAND STILL

Everything you do with your puppy, both on and off the lead, in the early days of his life will shape the individual he will become. The smallest cues, postures, and interactions that you share will help structure the way your pup views and responds to stimuli. The first days and weeks of his life in your home are a great time to get your dog into a receptive, learning state of mind.

A valuable skill that you should begin teaching your pup at an early age is to be calm and to stand still when being touched. In order to teach this skill efficiently and effectively, you must first be calm yourself. As noted above, dogs are incredibly adept at picking up on our emotional state, and their behavior is often a reflection of our mindset, posture, and tone. If you primarily love on your pup when he stands still, he will soon realize that standing still like a gentleman is a good way to get attention. If you can communicate this philosophy to the family and incorporate a standard expectation of behavior when handling the pup on a day-to-day basis, members of your family—and all folks, for that matter—will have a much easier time handling the pup as he grows up. Being calm includes the voice and energy that you use around the dog. An excited way of moving and a high-pitched, excited voice will impart excitement to your pup and encourage unwanted movement.

The first puppy that our twins, Reagan and Gage, considered their own was a pointer female named Faith. She was a very friendly pup, but she developed a severe case of the bounces whenever she was around people. Whenever she was near our kids, she got incredibly excited, and she regularly bumped them and accidentally knocked them over. We began working diligently on this behavior when Faith was about 12 weeks old. We held her gently and calmly by the collar until she had all four feet on the ground and was settled, both mentally and physically. As soon as she settled, we calmly rubbed on her as a reward. We kept our demeanor and our actions deliberate and slow. As a result of modeling this consistent behavioral expectation, the kids were quickly able to hold Faith to the same standard. Just like us, they held Faith gently by the collar and rewarded her desirable behavior with attention and praise. Due to this handling and the expectations

that were established early on, our kids did not become overwhelmed by the inadvertent damage of an overexuberant puppy, and Faith proved easier to train and easier to handle for life. The ability to stand calm and still is a characteristic that makes a dog more appreciated throughout its life.

NURTURING YOUR PUP'S NATURAL RETRIEVE

Even when the dog is young, you can begin to cultivate specific behaviors that will be of benefit in the field. It's good to start building your puppy's natural retrieve ability early on, so be certain to encourage and reward your pup when he picks up a bumper or toy. Don't ask him to give it to you immediately; just give him some "attaboys" and attention first. This will help keep the retrieve from becoming a game of possession.

A hallway is a good place to start encouraging a retrieve, as there is little to distract your puppy in the narrow space that creates a direct line for the pup to pick up the object and come back to you. Throw short retrieves at first and try to keep it fun. As your puppy matures and his desire to retrieve increases, you can build up the amount of time you spend doing retrieve work. Once your puppy is pretty good at retrieving in the hallway, progress to doing the same thing in the backyard with your puppy on a rope. The rope will help you to guide him back to you should he want to take a winner's lap around the yard. Work to keep him coming straight back to you without deviation.

If you get in a situation where he is retrieving while he does not have a rope on, resist the temptation to chase or follow him if he does not come to you. Following your dog in this way can evolve into a game of keep-away after a retrieve, and your pup may become intimidated and begin to spit out what he has in his mouth. If your pup moves away on a retrieve and you do not have a way of guiding him back in, just stop the game. If he doesn't bring the dummy back, the game is over. If this situation arises, you will need to make a mental note that in the future, you will need a drag line so that you can cue him to come to you, reshaping his delivery.

There are some things to watch out for when you are working to build the natural retrieve. Squeaky toys can have their place and can entice a reluctant retriever to pick up an object and play with it. That said, watch your dog to make sure that in biting to cause the toy to squeak, he does not become excited about biting and focused on destroying the retrieved object. What your pup does to a toy in the early days will likely predict his behavior with real birds later on. Another obvious behavior to watch out for is the desire for a retrieve and delivery to turn into a game of tug-of-war. You never want to encourage this behavior as it too will encourage the destruction of birds later on. Keep the end result in mind even as you play in the backyard.

We are not touching on a trained retrieve, or "force fetch," in the scope of this book. That training requires a book unto itself. We do encourage you to work with your budding bird dog's natural retrieve and keep it positive. Remember, the pup is retrieving only because he wants to—if retrieving becomes a chore, he simply won't do it naturally. Keep retrieving fun and be a cheerleader for him.

BEGIN TEACHING YOUR PUP PROBLEM-SOLVING SKILLS

As your pup is assimilating into his new home, family, and schedule—it is a great time to begin to teach him how to problem-solve. The ability to problem-solve is an essential skill for any animal or person who hopes to succeed with training of any sort. Begin to teach problem-solving with short exercises incorporated into the general routine and scattered throughout the day. A good opportunity to work on problem-solving arises at meal times, when you can allow your pup to eat his meal only after he stands still like a gentleman. Be patient with this lesson, as it may take some time, and celebrate the small successes. The first time you attempt this exercise, it may take five full minutes to get the pup to stand still and he may only stand still for a second. As soon as he does stand still, put his bowl down and let him eat. Bit by bit, he will realize that the more quickly he stands still, the sooner he gets his food. Once he figures out how to wait patiently

for a meal, you can progress to other challenges. Try not letting him through an open door until he stands still, or try making him wait in the crate before being allowed to exit—all of these exercises reinforce the calm and patience we want to see in a good canine citizen.

As your pup grows older, the complexity of the challenges you present can increase a bit. Think of these challenges as conditioning exercises for your dog's mind, opportunities to build and refine the pup's problem-solving skill set. We utilize an agility course throughout our dogs' careers to challenge them mentally and physically and to keep them in a learning state of mind. You can begin challenging your dog with small obstacles, agility courses to navigate, and an unlimited range of lessons in patience and restraint. All are great for young dogs, provided the growing pup is not overly challenged physically. The greater the degree of mental engagement and resilience that can be cultivated at an early age, the more successful and confident the dog will be in the long-term—and the stronger the trainer-dog relationship will be as a result.

RECOMMENDED EQUIPMENT FOR PUPPIES

When preparing for the arrival of your pup, make sure you have the following equipment ready:

> **Flat leather collar with an extended D-ring.** An extended D-ring makes it easier to snap a lead in to a collar. We prefer this over an O-ring because the D-ring allows the collar to maintain it's circular shape around a dog's neck, rather than collapsing in a V-shape when the dog is pulling.

> **Lead with a snap**

> **Crate**

> **Water and Food Bowls**

> **A consistent, high-quality puppy or all life stage food, such as Purina Pro Plan Sport**

///

BUILDING BEHAVIORS AND EXPERIENCE IN THE FIELD

Letting young dogs become comfortable in the environment in which they are expected to perform later in life gives them an advantage. Animals that become conditioned to a mowed, manicured back lawn may never be fully comfortable navigating brush and cover in the pursuit of game birds. To make an equivalence, if you drop a bird-dog trainer in the middle of Manhattan, that trainer may be able to blunder around and accomplish his goals, but he or she will not be as efficient, effective, or confident as someone who was raised in the city. There are, after all, few similarities between the streets of Manhattan and bird-dog training fields.

Though it seems logical that an owner or trainer might set out to develop the skills of navigating authentic terrain in a young pup, we actually find that this process is frequently overlooked. When we think about the importance of introducing animals to realistic terrain, we often recall a group of young horses that Susanna's family bought straight off the racetrack and brought back to their West Texas ranch. Those horses had lived their young lives in flat paddocks and had run almost exclusively on flat manicured tracks. Susanna's family worked with the horses in pens to get their basic, foundational training in place, but when they first began riding the horses in the rough West Texas pasture, it was apparent that none of the animals had ever negotiated their way through rocks, brush, or cactus. Riding through the pasture on the ex-racehorses, the riders were on pins and needles, as any given rider never knew when his or her horse might stumble on a rock or run through a bush

instead of maneuver around it or even throw on the brakes and stop to avoid running into a cactus. The ranch was a foreign environment to those horses, and they were not mentally prepared to handle its challenges. It took time for those horses to become comfortable and sure-footed in that environment, and it hampered their ability to become dependable ranch horses.

The similarities between bird dogs and those ranch horses may not be immediately apparent, but consider the fact that pups experienced in desert terrain often come back from a lark in the outdoors with little or no damage to their bodies. They have learned over a lifetime of conditioning which plants they should avoid and which they can run right through. A dog with ample experience in an environment knows where to place his feet, and, in the long run, this dog will have fewer injuries. The poor pup that has never encountered desert terrain but is asked to navigate it as a hard-going adult will come

Give your young dog the opportunity to become comfortable in the environments that you will ask them to perform in later in life.

back to the house with cactus spines from eyebrow to tail-tip—it will surely take him some precious time and bloodshed to learn when to pick his way through rough spots and how to avoid injury. Until he has learned how to handle the terrain, this pup will not be a proficient bird finder; there will simply be too many factors other than birds that he will have to deal with mentally.

To avoid this long-term challenge, allocate some time to letting your puppy roam in the field. Let him chase butterflies and meadowlarks, let him learn to swim in the creek, and let him figure out how to pull burrs from his fur on his own. As the pup explores his work environment, he will rapidly input valuable data. The more knowledgeable and comfortable a young pup can become in the field, the easier he will be to train and the more effectively he will hunt later on.

It can be somewhat intimidating to consider letting your young pup off the lead to simply run untethered in the field. To raise a dog that follows your direction of travel naturally in the field, it is necessary to develop this skill with the young pup. If you put a puppy down in a field and just start walking, the pup will naturally want to go with you. If you watch a mama dog in the pasture with her pups, you will notice that she doesn't change her agenda much and doesn't spend a great deal of energy corralling her pups. She won't stop or circle back or change direction just because one pup has his nose stuck in a gopher hole and another is chasing a butterfly. The mama dog typically just keeps heading the way she wants to head, and eventually all the pups follow along. Take note of this tendency as you begin to put your pup down in the field, and also take note of the tendency we owners have to follow our dogs for fear that we might lose them.

When we take a litter of young puppies for their first walk in the field at Ronnie Smith Kennels, we try to find an easy place for them to walk with us, either a mowed field or a trail. We walk at a steady pace, and if one pup gets lost from the pack, we give him a locator call—usually "pup, pup, pup, pup,"—until he is able to find the group again. We don't say anything else until another pup needs a little redirecting, and then we give that locator call again. This process helps the pups learn to keep an eye out for the pack leader and go with him. Until they grow up a little and begin roaming a bit farther, they will typically fall behind the leader, and that's just fine for this early stage in life.

Remember not to talk too much to your pup out in the field. Give him a locator to help him when he needs it, but not much more. You will want to begin building a quiet presence in the field. Look into the future a bit and consider how you want to hunt with your pup down the line. Noise in the field scares wildlife off and makes a hunt less successful. A quiet atmosphere is more enjoyable for all involved, and hunters will be more likely to see game.

Remember that you are forming something of a pack with your new pup, and you are the pack leader. Remember, *you* get to decide which direction you will walk in the field, not the pup. These early walks with your pup establish the dynamics that will play out in your later excursions. Don't chase your pup or you will find yourself chasing him for life! Be the omniscient parent that calmly walks on while helping the young ones come too. Your body movement and posture provide your young dog with direction in these moments; if you move steadily on and keep the distractible pup's attention with a verbal "hey, pup, pup, pup," the pup is going to think that he had better catch up because the pack is on the move. He will almost invariably hustle to catch up with you. We often walk entire litters, sometimes two litters at a time, with ease by employing this way of handling. If you start this process with a young pup and continue the process as the pup grows, he will naturally think about going with you—at a greater distance—as a juvenile and then as an adult. Our goal is to have dogs that naturally go with us, remaining aware of where we are at all times while they go about doing their own job of hunting for birds.

Bear in mind that going with us does not mean following; it simply means that the pup or pups will key off our intended direction and not take over the steering wheel. At eight weeks of age, the pup that is going with you may actually be a pup

that is running about 20 feet behind you. At 16 weeks of age that same pup may be going with you by running 20 yards ahead of you and chasing butterflies, but nonetheless keeping an eye on you and changing direction to stay in line with you. At a year of age that same individual may range at 150 yards, but be savvy enough to look around for you, monitoring your progress and always staying to the front while also remaining focused on finding game. Dogs that are raised this way are typically rather hard to lose in the field as mature dogs.

On a final note, in order for a dog to effectively go with you in the field, that dog does not have to come back to you frequently to "check in." In fact, a dog that ranges out while hunting, but comes all the way back to you to check in is not as focused as he should be and will likely perform at about half the efficacy of a proficient hunter. It is our goal to maximize efficiency and effectiveness in our mature dogs, and this means that we allow dogs to range at the distance they are comfortable and not come back to check in unless they are specifically asked to do so or if the situation otherwise calls for it.

INTRODUCTION TO BIRDS

One of the most exciting moments with a young pup is watching him develop the passion for birds that foreshadows the great moments that an owner and dog will have in the field for years to come. At this stage, you start to see glimpses of what lies ahead, and you can really begin to visualize yourself with your new hunting partner. This is a significant moment in a dog's life—how it is structured can shape behavior for the entire training process, as well as the life of the dog.

Successful introduction to birds can take place once your pup is at least 10 weeks old and has become comfortable navigating easy pathways and short grass in the field. The best way to introduce your pup to birds is to have him encounter either a dead bird—a pigeon or quail is often what we use—or a live bird that has been placed in a simple harness and therefore cannot flap or move too erratically. It is important that the first several birds that the pup investigates do not flap their wings in the

pup's face or fly up with a sudden movement. The goal is to create a situation that builds confidence around birds; we do not want to allow a situation to occur that will cause fear in the pup.

When introducing your pup to birds, keep sessions short and expectations realistic. Puppies, even

One of the most exciting moments with a young pup is watching him develop the passion for birds that foreshadows the great moments that an owner and dog will have in the field.

those who go on to become bird-finding machines, are likely to respond to initial bird exposure in a variety of ways. Puppies are likely to either act scared of the bird at first, be indifferent toward it, or circle it and bark without going in to investigate. These are all perfectly normal and acceptable responses to initial exposure, and none should be cause for concern. Remember, you are introducing a new animal to your puppy, and as with all new stimuli, the pup has to size it up and process the situation thoroughly before he can feel comfortable. If your puppy remains indifferent and walks away from the bird, it is certainly acceptable to wiggle, toss, or shake the bird a bit to help stir the pup's natural prey drive. Most likely, this bit of movement will stimulate the chase response, and your pup will probably chase after the bird without even thinking about it. Don't feel the need to force the issue with your pup. If he walks away from the bird after a few moments, that is okay. Rest assured that once the genetically ingrained prey drive takes over—and it almost invariably will—the pup will be hooked on all things related to birds. Give your pup the opportunity to progress at his pace, and he will blossom.

Once your pup has shown significant interest in birds he can see, you can start hiding birds in the grass, provided the grass is not too tall or thick for your puppy to navigate easily. The primary goal during bird introduction is to keep the pup successful. Be confident, and progress with small steps; don't challenge the pup too much at first. Once he begins to show signs that he is using his nose to locate birds in thicker cover, and once he begins to go in on a bird to confidently get his mouth on it, then you can start introducing released birds, or birds that are not restrained. We typically like to use the sorriest quail in our bird pens for this purpose, as they are not strong fliers and will generally not flush too aggressively, nor will they fly far after the flush. A flush and flight of about 10 to 20 yards is ideal. This way, your puppy can learn to mark a bird down and relocate it. Also, you can get a lot of good bird work on just a few birds.

If your pup begins to catch some birds, don't panic. Try not to act upset about the bird being caught and instead keep your demeanor positive. If a bird is caught, use the opportunity to work on bringing your dog in for a good retrieve. Kneel down and call your dog to help bring him in on a direct line to you. After that bird session is complete, change gears and get some better flying birds. Remember, catching some birds is not necessarily a bad thing—you just don't want it to become commonplace.

Because the philosophy behind The Smith Training Method is based on taking a dog's natural instinct and nurturing it with minimal human interference, we allow the pups to search and find the planted birds with minimal coaching and minimal verbal commands. In our experience, verbal commands, encouragement, or physical gestures can distract the pup from using his nose to search out a bird, thereby interfering with the natural lesson. If your pup casts out in a direction opposite from where you know the bird to be, you may walk a few steps in the direction of the bird to help cast him back. If he runs completely out of the scenario, you can then give him a verbal reference—"hup" or "ho" or "pup," etc.—to simply steer his attention back into the general zone of the bird. When you are in the vicinity of

a bird, you should try to keep language and motion to a minimum so that the pup can do what his instincts tell him to do.

During this initial stage of bird introduction, *the pup can do no wrong.* Do not worry if your pup chases a bird, catches a bird, plays with a bird, or fails to showcase a classic point. Everything is a positive, reinforced by the genetic prey drive that was put into the pup through sound breeding. At this stage, all that matters is that the pup develops a passion for using its nose to find game. If a pup "rips" a bird out of cover and chases, it does not mean that the pup will never become a good pointer. The focus in these initial sessions is to bring the inherent prey drive to a pinnacle; manners will come later during formal training.

At Ronnie Smith Kennels, our philosophy on early bird introduction is that naturally occurring wild-bird encounters are always preferable. That said, like so many rules of bird-dog training, the wild-bird rule is riddled with caveats. At times, your pup may struggle to catch their scent, and therefore the contact won't substantively build prey drive. It is common when working in wild-bird country that a beautiful covey of birds gets up right in the thick of a group of pups—and not a single pup is aware of their presence. Pup #1 may be rolling in the mud, pup #2 chewing on #1's lead, and pup #3 chasing a grasshopper. No matter how carefully you set up your pups for effective bird exposures, situations like this arise. Under such circumstances, all you can do is smile at your pups' youth and proceed as if nothing negative has happened, which, in the pups' world, is true! Next time, try to set up a more controlled environment, like putting the puppy on a check cord so that you can place him in the scent cone and a bird in a tip-up.

To illustrate this point, when Rock and Grace were about five months old, we worked them on wild quail. Grace quickly became a bird-seeking missile; after a few contacts, all she could think about when her feet hit the ground was finding birds. Her brother, on the other hand, could not get puppy play out of his mind. If he was on the ground alone, he was eating cow poop, chasing grasshop-

Even though your pup may sit in the middle of the road while birds call all around him, be patient and continue to present him with learning opportunities.

pers, looking for a stick to carry, or picking the stickers out of his feet. If he was running with Grace, he was focused intently on dogging her, far more aware of his sister than of the birds she was intent on finding. He was blissfully unaware of the wild quail that flushed all around him. His workouts in Texas were of minimal benefit to him, because the opportunity for wild-bird contacts simply didn't line up in a way that got his attention. Despite some missed opportunities, we were not concerned. Rock just needed a different set of circumstances to really get focused and become a great wild-bird dog. He needed controlled exposure to planted birds, and he needed to be check-corded into the scent cone in order to become focused. Wild birds, while great for his sister, simply did not provide the best opportunity to enhance Rock's early development and prey drive.

It is important not to get frustrated with pups. They will blossom at their own speed. A love for the game is something you cannot force. Keep giving them opportunities on birds, and their true genetic potential will surface. If your workout does not go according to plan or your pup just is not fired up yet, just resolve to keep creating learning opportunities for him as he continues to grow and mature. 🐾

RECOMMENDED EQUIPMENT FOR USE IN THE FIELD WITH YOUNG PUPS

As you venture into the field to expose your pup to birds, there is some necessary equipment that you should have on hand. The following is a basic assortment of tools that are readily available from several sporting-dog suppliers:

❯ **Drag Line** – When running puppies, we frequently use puppy drag lines. These are roughly 10-foot leads of light cord with a snap at one end and no knots on the other. The concept of the drag line is to provide a "handle" that can be easily reached if you need to catch your pup and cue him to you. Drag lines can also be grabbed and used to silently cast a dog in a certain direction to ensure his success.

❯ **Tip Up** – When working pups on pen-raised birds, we often use a tip-up. A tip-up is simply a small wire cage that holds a bird in place while leaving it exposed to the air, allowing its scent to escape. The tip-up has an angled bar or metal loop welded onto it that acts as a lever; when a trainer steps on the lever, the cage portion tips up and the bird can release. A tip-up allows a timid pup to get close to the bird to investigate before it flies away. Conversely, a bolder dog that rushes in on scent can get close to the planted bird without the danger of a remote bird releaser deploying in his face and scaring him.

❯ **Birds** – When introducing birds in the initial phases, a dead or frozen bird, a wing-tied pigeon, or quail will suffice. In general, pigeons are heartier than quail and seem to kick off a powerful scent for a young dog. Do be aware that a flushing pigeon creates quite a disturbance, and wings should be tied or harnessed to ensure that a pup doesn't get spooked by a face-full of flapping wings.

❯ **Check cord** – If your dog needs a little extra guidance to learn to work scent, snap a check cord into his collar and cast him across the scent cone. A check cord is a rigid cord that has enough structure for the trainer to grasp and deliver cues to the dog.

2

//////////////////////////////////

FORMAL
TRAINING

When should formal training begin? A dog is typically ready for formal training when he is approximately one year of age, he has shown himself mature enough mentally to focus on a task for a period of time, and his prey drive is at a pinnacle. Ideally, a dog that is entering the formal training process has become "bird crazy" and all that he can think about when turned loose is locating game. This sort of behavior typically coincides with or indicates that a pup is confident on his own and is no longer paying much attention to his owner in the field.

The least important indicator of a dog's readiness for formal training is the dog's age. Many of our young pups have had lots of bird and real-world exposure and have been ready for formal training well before they reached a year of age. Starting these dogs a bit younger is fine as long as you keep their age in mind and do not push them past their physical and mental limits. Frequently, we encounter dogs that are a year old or more and yet have not experienced sufficient bird and real-world exposure to prepare them for training. Even if a dog is two- or three-years-old, he may not be ready for formal training until he has had the exposure necessary to maximize his prey drive and give him a high degree of comfort in the field.

When we receive dogs for training, we evaluate them in the field to see if they are prepared for formal training. We use the first few moments we spend with a dog as a snapshot of their emotional well-being and preparedness for training. Since we approach these dogs with a clean slate, we are able to pick out and flag certain behaviors that may impact the dog's success in both formal training and in life.

The first characteristic we check on is the dog's degree of socialization. When we, as strangers, walk up to the dog, we want him to be receptive to us. If the dog has not been properly socialized, he will not be receptive to us approaching him, touching him, and eventually working with him. Poor socialization will place an immediate hurdle in front of both the trainer and the dog, and therefore time and effort must be allocated to socialization before more training can begin. A dog that is properly socialized and therefore receptive to training will acknowledge his trainer and be friendly.

The second characteristic we evaluate is prey drive. We snap a check cord to the dog's collar, and we quarter him out into the field. If the dog begins using his nose and working the terrain in search of birds, he is ready to begin formal training. Ideally, we want a dog to show us that he can use the wind to work scent and establish an intense point when he determines there is a bird ahead of him.

There is a test we can use if we want to check for intensity once the dog has "made

game." It is not necessary to use this test; however, if you are uncertain if your dog has enough focus and intensity on game, this can be utilized. With the dog on point or otherwise focused on a planted bird, we use a slow, gentle tug on the check cord. If the dog disengages with the planted bird immediately and either turns his head away from the bird to look at us or walks toward us, we know there are some issues that need to be dealt with. In this situation, we typically either need to further develop the dog's prey drive or we need to "erase" established human fingerprints that have managed to override the dog's inherent prey drive. If the dog does not budge or acknowledge the tension on the check cord, we can be confident that he is focused on the bird and ready to begin his formal training.

This "intensity check" is a gauge that we use once and only once during the dog's initial evaluation. It is a tool that enables us to rapidly gain insight to the dog's state of mind and to gauge how the dog will respond during training. If we are familiar with a dog, we do not use this intensity test because that snapshot report about the dog's intensity is not necessary.

Though it can be tempting to periodically gauge a dog's level of intensity, we do not recommend putting a dog through this exercise for any reason or at any time other than a one-time assessment of readiness for training. This test is designed to intentionally gauge what degree of pressure it will take to break a dog's focus on game—and in repeating this process, you might eventually teach your dog that you want him to break on game. Our primary goal in training is to keep the dog keenly focused on a bird, and therefore breaking off scent is a behavior that a trainer should not teach!

While we are evaluating a dog to see if they are ready for formal training, we look for cues about how mentally mature the dog is. In general, this requires that we look at a dog's ability to maintain focus. If a dog is looking for a bird one moment and chewing on a stick the next, we know that the dog may lack some maturity, and therefore may easily be distracted from the training at hand. This is a dog that may benefit from a little more time to mature before starting a formal training program.

A dog that is intent on finding game, receptive to his trainer, and mature enough to stay focused during a workout exhibits the requisites to be considered ready to begin his formal training.

PREREQUISITES FOR FORMAL TRAINING:

› Good social skills › High prey drive and intensity on birds › Mature mindset

THE FOUNDATION LEVEL OF TRAINING

The Foundation Level of training serves as the hub of the entire training format. Everything taught throughout the rest of the format is developed from the elements instilled at this level.

The Smith Training Method is broken down into three distinct separate levels of training: the Foundation Level, the Intermediate Level, and the Advanced Level. For us, each level of training equals roughly a month of working with a dog every day. While a dog's training is truly never complete, this format allows us to get a dog through the basic training within 90 days. After this 90-day class, dogs are ready to transition to hunting scenarios. We do encourage more practice at the Advanced Level prior to field trialing, but the basic training will result in a proficient "rookie" bird dog.

The Foundation Level of training serves as the hub of the entire training format. Everything taught throughout the rest of the format is developed from the elements instilled at this level. Just as in building a house, the quality of the entire structure depends on the quality of the foundation. We prefer to spend as much time as necessary to perfect behavior at this level of training because it will mean the rest of training typically will go more smoothly.

The Foundation Level begins to develop the basic behaviors that will be applied throughout a dog's life, both in the home as well as in the hunting field. Put in very elementary terms, every dog should *come to you, stand still, and go with you*.

This is also the period during which points of contact are established to communicate to a dog. Points of contact are certain spots on the body that are referenced to cue dogs to give certain conditioned responses. Through repetition, dogs develop conditioned responses to specific cues for the three basic behaviors—come to you, stand still, and go with you.

Once we have moved through this level and established those cues and responses with a dog, we are able to move into the Intermediate Level of training. At this point, we can easily transition from the mechanical cues of a rope to low-level remote cues of the training collar to achieve the same response. We utilize a training collar on the flank to begin stopping a dog in the Intermediate Level of training. Through the Intermediate Level, we begin turning dogs loose in the field, and subsequently we are able to begin the steadying process on live birds. Once our dogs have been steadied on pigeons and have developed a sound understanding of the cues of the training collar, we move on to the Advanced Level of training. In the Advanced Level, all cues are moved to the neck, field work transitions to a focus on game birds, and we begin shooting birds over our dogs. At the Advanced Level, we practice to the point of learned behavior.

Our Foundation Training consists of two sessions each day. One session concentrates on obedience— learning to respond to light cues of a rope or lead, heeling, recall, whoa, and generally being mannerly. The second session during the Foundation daily schedule consists of bird work on a check cord in the field, where we focus on building prey drive, developing behavior around birds, and introducing backing scenarios, or scenarios where a trailing dog must 'honor' a dog that has established point. It is not nec-

essary to break up the training in exactly this way, but we do strongly encourage you to balance obedience training with bird work. It is often easier to concentrate on obedience first and then factor in the field work when you can. However, this approach often costs the trainer a bit more time, as the dog's obedience develops to the point that he is ready to move on to the Intermediate Level, but his bird exposure and desire is not strong enough for him to be successful at the lessons involved in the Intermediate Level of training. As you move through the Foundation Level, keep a mental note of how many obedience sessions you've done and how much bird work you've been able to accomplish. If one area gets ahead of the other, try to even out the balance again.

STRUCTURING YOUR TRAINING SESSION

When structuring a training session, it is good to follow a few simple principles:

> Every time you work with your dog, you should have a goal in mind. There should always be at least one lesson that you want to accomplish with each workout. The goal can be a physical behavior or response, or it could be to simply get the dog to enter a receptive, calm, trainable state of mind. Identify your main goal before the workout and tailor your workout to accomplish that end.

> Keep your workouts short. A short, but effective workout is more beneficial to your dog's education than a long workout that may wear your dog out mentally. A 15-minute workout can be plenty if you maintain focus and accomplish a goal during that time.

> Always end the lesson on a positive note. Get something accomplished, make sure your dog is in a good state of mind, and then end the session.

RECOMMENDED EQUIPMENT FOR FOUNDATION LEVEL OF TRAINING

> **Leather collar with extended D-ring**
> **20-foot check cord**
> **Tie-out** for your dog while you set up exercises
> **Water and bowl** for your dog
> **Pigeons** and a method of restraining them, such as a tip-up, to successfully plant them in the field
> **Up to three soft 20-foot ropes** with swivel snaps

on both ends for Whoa Post workouts (to be covered in this section), and **secure stakes** to serve as the posts
> **Command Lead** (a.k.a. the Wonder Lead, which will also be discussed in this section)
> **Bird bag**

UNDERSTANDING CUES, ACKNOWLEDGMENTS, AND COMPLIANCE

//

Before beginning formal training, it is important to understand the fundamentals of what constitutes a cue and how to gauge a dog's understanding of cues through compliance and acknowledgments. When you begin to really study a dog's behavior, you will become ultra-aware that there are cues and acknowledgments already built into your daily life together.

A cue is any stimulus that achieves a reaction or response from an animal. A cue that you already may have incorporated into your daily life with your dog might be the noise of opening the dog food container. This is a stimulus that calls your dog to the kitchen. Also, the cue of picking up a leash may cause your dog to rush to the door, expecting a walk outside.

Cues that are the most useful in training can be audible, visual, or physical. An example of an audible cue is a spoken word or a whistle. A physical cue can be a touch from a handler, the mechanical touch of a rope or lead, or the remote cue of a training collar. Visual cues can look like the motion of holding your hand out palm-first to indicate you want your dog to stop. In order for a visual cue to work, however, your dog has to be looking at the cue, which is not always possible in the field with pointing dogs.

We use all types of cues in our training, however we always begin teaching through the use of physical cues. From there we are able to label known, established behaviors with audible or visual cues. We wait to use audible or visual cues until after the behavior is learned and perfected through

a conditioned response to a physical cue, so that we do not improperly label the wrong behavior. For example, if you begin saying "whoa" before your dog has a conditioned response to a physical cue to stop, you are liable to find yourself in a scenario where you are saying "whoa, whoa, whoa, whoa, whoa, whoa…" and do not have an established way of physically enforcing the behavior. This creates confusion for the dog as to what exactly you mean when you say "whoa." Does "whoa" mean walk slowly, mill around, or stop on the 26th "whoa"? The audible cue has been poisoned and will lack effective meaning to the dog.

Through repetition during our Foundation Level of training, we are able to establish a conditioned response to a physical cue, and from that point forward, we are able to reference the physical cue to enforce behavior quickly and easily. After a conditioned response to a physical cue is developed, then we can successfully factor in visual and audible cues and gain compliance.

Some of the physical cues that we use during the Foundation Level of training are a pull and release on a point of contact on a dog through the use of a rope. An example is teaching a dog to respond or "give" to the mechanical cue on the neck. A leash or a check cord is used to apply slight pressure on the dog's neck. When the dog gives or yields to that pressure, it is quickly released. This is how animals learn to respond to a physical cue in a way that turns it off. The reward for the animal is the release of the cue. This can easily be seen when teaching a puppy to lead. In order to get the pup to go a

//

certain direction, pressure is applied to the rope. When that pup moves in the desired direction, he automatically gains a release, and this teaches the pup how to turn off the stimuli. In rapid succession, the puppy learns to move when cued mechanically on the neck. This basic scenario can be expanded to include a myriad of behaviors, including stopping, coming to you, and going with you.

In order for any cue to be effective, the dog being cued has to be aware of the cue. This is where one of our favorite mantras comes into play: *The level of distraction dictates the level of intensity.* This simply means that any cue given has to be obvious enough that the dog can be aware of it in the context of the training environment. The analogy that we often use employs the different states of mind between people reading in a library and people in the stands at a football game. If you are studying philosophy in a library, your friend may be able to whisper or just barely touch your arm to break your focus from your studies. However, if you are at your favorite

football team's championship game and the action is high, a holler and a hard pull on your sleeve may be necessary to just break your attention away from the game. It is the same for a dog. A dog in a controlled, quiet environment will likely be aware of a very light cue. However, the same dog a moment later as he chases a bird, cat, or squirrel may not be aware of the same cue at all; it would take a much higher-level cue to gain an awareness.

Once you become aware of distinct cues you are already using in your day-to-day life, you will likely be amazed at the acknowledgments that your dog is already giving you, indicating his understanding. An acknowledgment can be shown in many ways, the most common being yawning, licking, or swallowing.

Have you ever stood quietly at a door and waited patiently for a dog to calm down before you let him outside? If you have, then you've probably seen an acknowledgment. Your dog likely bounced around in excitement for a few minutes and then began to

try to figure out what he could do to be let outside. After assessing the situation, he most likely acknowledged what he needed to do and complied by standing by your side, at which time he yawned or licked his lips.

We see the same acknowledgments throughout our training. Over the years we have learned that by waiting for an acknowledgment from a dog, we give him time to think through the lesson and figure out what we are asking of him. Allowing a dog the time to think through things helps speed the training format as a whole and clarifies lessons for dogs. We look for acknowledgments in everything we do with dogs, but they become a critical part of teaching a dog on the Whoa Post, which we will talk about in depth later on.

Once you begin noticing acknowledgments, the moment that a dog makes the decision to comply with a stimulus will become much more apparent to you. For example, in teaching a dog to recall, you may go through the process of cue, wait for the acknowledgment, and then see the compliance as the dog makes the decision and walks toward you. Beginning to pay attention to these nuances helps any trainer to learn how better to communicate with a dog, and how to teach him in a clear manner.

When a dog makes the decision not to comply with a cue, he often simply continues with what he is doing without much change in his body language. One exception to that rule occurs when a dog "shakes it off." You will often see this behavior after cueing a dog to do something that he does not want to do. He may simply shrug off the cue by shaking as if just he'd just stepped out of a pool of water. The analogous human behavior is that of a person thinking "I don't care what that was, and it did not affect me." If you see your dog shake off a cue, make a mental note that he has not fully joined up with you and you may need some extra time in your workouts to find the right mix of cues to get him in a better, more receptive, and trainable state of mind.

THE CLASSROOM SETTING: THE TIE-OUT

Throughout our training process, we use a tie-out as a method of keeping multiple dogs near at hand in the field, and keeping them safe and orderly as a group. The tie-out also teaches some simple lessons in yielding to cues. A tie-out is a set of stakes in the ground connected by a cable or a short chain off of which a dropper chain is snapped to the extended D-ring in the dog's flat collar. Often, multiple dogs are spread out down the length of one long master chain that is staked on either end, essentially with short dropper lines extending at even intervals, far enough apart to keep dogs physically separated.

We think of dogs on a tie-out as something akin to kids in a classroom. The tie-out is where we put our entire class of dogs each morning before their workouts. There are myriad benefits that stem from having your dog on a tie-out during training. First, being placed on the tie-out marks the beginning of class. Second, the tie-out it is a secure and safe place for a dog to settle and wait—and to learn to wait patiently. Most importantly, a tie-out is a place where a dog can continue the lesson of cue-and-release that was started by the lead rope. The tie-out creates a clear introduction to cues—when the dog feels a cue on his neck, he learns to give to the pressure in order to gain a release. By virtue of physics, the tie-out will never fail to give that cue and is a consistent trainer. Without even thinking about learning, the dog is learning to respond to a cue on the neck.

In the Smith family we have a saying, "anything built for a dog should be built for a horse."

This refers to the fact that dog equipment should be strong enough to withstand a horse's amount of strength. Dogs will put any and all equipment to the test, so set up tie-outs to be sturdy enough that you don't look up one day to see your dog high-tailing it across the field when he should be safe and asleep at his tie-out. To build a tie-out, we recommend starting with a 7/16 plastic-coated cable or a chain. Cable is light, durable, and easy to pack. It has become our preference when traveling. Tie-outs can be made to hold up to five or six dogs at a time. Begin by tying or fastening an O-Ring on each end of the long cable. A tie-out lead can come off this main bottom cable at approximately 6-foot intervals, depending on the average size of your dog. Tie-outs should be designed to have enough space between each dog that they cannot nose each other or fight, and therefore bigger dogs will need slightly more space between the leads. *Be certain to have double-end swivels at the bottom of each tie-out lead, as well as a swivel snap at the top.* This will help ensure a dog does not get twisted in the line. We strongly recommend always using swivels when dealing with ropes or tie-outs of any sort for any animal.

The tie-out leads themselves should be only slightly longer than the distance from the ground to your dog's collar. The dogs should be able to stand with no tension on the lead. Conversely there should not be so much slack in the leads that the dogs find themselves tangled up. If all your dogs are Weimaraners, your tie-outs should be longer than those of the person who has only French Brittanys.

When looking for a suitable spot to place your

TIE OUT

tie-out, look for a piece of level ground in the shade that is far enough away from fences or structures that your dog cannot become entangled in or chew. When you have the spot selected, put the sharp tip of your first stake through the O-ring at the end of your tie-out and use a sledge to secure the stake 18 to 24 inches in the ground. Check to make sure it is firm, as wet ground can prove less stable than you'd think!

Once the first end of the tie-out is secured, stretch the main line of the tie-out along the ground in the direction you'd like it to run, and drive your second stake through the O-ring on the other end. Keep tension on the cable and drive your stake into the ground while it is angled back toward the tie-out; after the stake has bit into the ground, you can push it over to create added tension on the main line. Ideally the stakes should stand at 45- to 60-degree angles out from the tie-out in order to help keep tension on the chains and prevent the O-rings from popping off over the top of the stake.

Remember whenever a tie-out is being used, make certain the dogs have shade and water. Do not leave dogs tied out and unsupervised!

GENERAL TIE-OUT DIMENSIONS FOR AN AVERAGE-SIZED DOG:

1) 6 feet between tie-out leads
2) 15- to 18-inch long tie-out leads
3) Up to 30 feet total length of central tie-out line
4) ¾-inch double-end swivel at the bottom, connecting the tie-out to the main line
5) ¾-inch swivel snap at the top of the tie-out lead

TEACH YOUR DOG TO "PRESENT" HIMSELF AT THE TIE-OUT

A lot can be gained by having your dog settle and stand calmly while being put on or taken off of a tie-out. For this reason, the tie-out is where our formal training usually begins. To have a dog learn to present himself, walk up to him, and stand beside him so that he is in the heeling position (a right-handed shooter keeps the dog on the left side).

The tie-out is a great training tool for all dogs. Each time a dog pulls on his drop-chain he feels a cue on the neck. The cue is released when he ceases to pull, and chooses to sit or stand calmly.

Wait until the dog quits bouncing around in excitement and is collected enough to "present himself," or stand calmly next to you. Stand on the main line of the tie-out where the drop chain connects, so that your dog cannot jump and hit your leg with the bouncing chain or cable. Be neutral with your body and attitude and wait for your dog to settle. He may jump around, sit, lie down, or have a big case of the wiggles—but a bit of time and a relaxed, calm demeanor on your part will help your dog settle his mind and stop moving. Once your dog is calm, still, and quiet, then you can reach down and attach the check cord to his flat collar.

If at any point during this process your dog slips out of that calm mindset and begins to wiggle, simply stop what you are doing and stand back up with your body calm and neutral. Your dog will quickly learn that he doesn't get to go anywhere or gain any attention until he stands still. With consistency, it will only take a few days for your dog to begin to stand calmly as soon as you approach him on the tie-out or in the kennel.

Once your dog is standing still by your side, reach down and snap a check cord to the D-ring on his collar, unhook the tie-out snap, and cue him to move forward. To cue a dog to move forward or "release," we give them a single light touch on the top of the dog's head. We utilize this cue at every opportunity to indicate a release during training. The more repetition the dog has, the sooner this will develop in to a deeply ingrained conditioned response.

These simple lessons that surround the more formal components of bird-dog training are quite valuable and will have limitless long-term benefits. A dog that stands calmly will be roundly appreciated by your vet at his next visit. Similarly, it will be far easier for you to handle, groom, and tend to your dog's physical needs and appearance if he is comfortable standing calmly in your presence. Your dog will be noted as a gentleman when people walk up to meet him, and he will stand beside you quietly when you talk with a friend. The list of benefits surrounding a foundation of calm and gentlemanly behavior goes on and on.

TEACH YOUR DOG TO BE CALM AND PRESENT HIMSELF IN EVERY SITUATION

Any time you put your hands on and handle your dog or work in close proximity to your dog, he should be able to stand politely and calmly, whether on a tie-out or not. This is not a trait that is inherent in all dogs and usually is one that takes time and effort to develop. Begin at the tie-out—a controlled environment where success will come quicker—and then progress to more challenging, uncontrolled environments.

Keep in mind that your energy always transfers to your dog. If your dog stands by your side calmly and you reach down and touch him in a fast, energetic manner and speak with lots of energy in your voice, you can cause him to fail. Your energy will cause him to move excitedly. Try to keep your voice and demeanor genuine and calm.

Use the technique applied at the tie-out and transition to requiring your dog to be calm by your side, no matter where you are or what you are doing. Use a leash correction instead of relying on the tie-out to do the work for you. Any time your dog bounces out of position, make a leash correction and bring him back in position.

By using a calm touch on your dog's shoulders, you can often help him to relax and stand still. This technique can be used any time your dog needs a little extra help relaxing and being still.

This is a good time to work on being able to run your hands all over your dog and get them used to standing still while you do so. Take this opportunity to develop the behavior of standing calmly while ears are being checked, teeth are examined, feet are picked up and held, and any areas your particular dog is sensitive to is empathetically touched. Try to desensitize your dog to being touched and worked with. Practice the behavior that will make it easier to place equipment on your dog, such as hunting vests, dog boots and training collars.

FIELD WORKOUTS

//

EQUIPMENT AND BIRDS

We begin our Foundation Level of training with bird work. During this month of training, we strive to balance bird work with obedience work. As you teach behaviors and cues, you also want to make certain that your dog's prey drive is at a pinnacle. Thus, we usually do a morning workout on birds and an afternoon obedience session each day. You may not be able to do both in the same day due to time constraints, but we do recommend keeping a balance between your bird workouts and obedience workouts.

The equipment you use in the field will vary depending on a few factors, specifically how much money you want to allocate to training equipment, how much help you have in the field, and what you have available for live training birds. When working with live birds in a field setting, you will need a method of holding a bird in place on the ground so that you can work your dog into it reliably. At Ronnie Smith Kennels, the equipment for holding birds changes as we go through the training progression. We usually begin working a dog in the field with tip-ups, or wire cages that are placed over the bird to hold it in place. In the context of dog-training equipment, tip-ups are relatively inexpensive to purchase. However, since they are not automated, tip-ups do require that you have a helper in the field with you to flush.

If you do not have a helper that can consistently be present to flush birds for you, a remote launcher is likely the best tool. Remote launchers are auto-

mated, spring-loaded metal boxes that launch a live bird at the push of a button on a remote controller. Remote launchers require a bit more financial investment on the part of the trainer, but they allow you to launch a bird remotely while you are working your dog, thereby allowing an individual the freedom to work a dog without assistance.

Your supply of live birds will also, to some degree, dictate your workouts. It is ideal when training to have steady access to pigeons, optimally a flock of homing pigeons that return to a loft near your training ground after each workout. A flock of homers allows you to work with the same pigeons day after day, without having to buy new ones regularly. That said, it takes a bit of an investment in time and infrastructure to get pigeons homing to their loft. Typically, we buy common pigeons and house them for four to six weeks, then slowly begin turning them loose for short flights, in which they return to the loft through a one-way door. Once pigeons are conditioned to fly back to their loft, they are an extremely valuable tool for training, and a good pigeon that homes back is worth his weight in gold. If you don't have the facility to house pigeons or the time to get them homing, you may need to buy birds every time you work your dog. You will certainly want to have a mesh bird bag with a spring-loaded opening and a shoulder strap to move birds around in the training field.

If possible, we recommend starting your training using common pigeons that are already homing to your loft. They are tough, hardy birds that are easy to care for and house. They are strong flyers that

//

The Foundation Level of training begins the process of shaping the behaviors desired in a bird dog, such as pointing, backing, and retrieving.

tend to flush and leave the area, rather than setting back down a short distance away, as some pen-raised game birds such as quail or chukar will do.

If pigeons cannot be located, pen-raised game birds can suffice, though it is not ideal to begin your formal training with game birds. Birds that do not fly completely out of the training field make training more difficult, as young dogs encounter workouts wherein birds can be caught. If a young dog feels that a bird can be crept on and caught, the process of instilling steadiness will go much more slowly. We also encourage the use of pigeons because if something should go wrong during train-ing—if for some reason your dog is feeling pressure on birds—you can often reinvigorate the prey drive by switching over to game birds. If you introduce live-bird training with game birds, you are out this ace in the hole. It's a good ace to have just in case you should ever need it.

The first stage in live-bird training is to check-cord your dog into pigeons in tip-ups. From there you will progress to working your dog into pigeons in launchers, and during the final stages of train-ing, your dog will make the transition to locating pen-raised game birds in launchers.

CHECK-CORDING

When we progress to the Foundation Level of bird work, we use the check cord to begin molding dogs' behavior on birds. We tailor their experience to set them up for success when they are doing the same things off the rope. We try to show them how to go with us and stay in front, work scent, stand through the flush, and honor another dog's point. This is also a great time to work on further building your dog's natural retrieve.

Check-cording also allows us to work both sides of an animal. As is the case with horses, dogs are often considered right-brain- or left-brain-oriented as individuals. As an example, a few summers ago we had a dog in for training that always pulled hard to the right when check-corded, and it was an effort to get him to complete his cast all the way to the left. By consistently requiring him to go the same distance to the left as we had asked him to go to the right, we were able to begin to work on evening out his pattern. During training, we continually made an effort to get this dog to complete his casts to the left. We were successful in doing so by walking him in that direction. When we moved him on to wild birds on the prairies, we had to address the issue again. By beginning to address it on the check cord, we laid a foundation that helped in addressing it when it came back in a different situation.

Functionally speaking, check-cording a dog is

pretty straightforward; all it requires is a field of open ground, a 20-foot check cord, and a flat leather collar. To make check-cording easier, we have identified some equipment features that stand out to us as important for efficiency and functionality.

Our leather collars are 21 inches long, as this size fits most bird-dog breeds. We prefer a strong leather flat collar because it is a durable natural product, but also because it rotates smoothly on the dog's neck and does not pull hair. We like our collars to have an extended D-ring to make attaching check cords and leads easy. We do not recommend collars that feature a central O-ring, as that type of collar collapses in to a V on the dog's neck while check-cording. When this occurs, the collar cannot rotate smoothly around the dog's neck, and the pinched V causes the dog to have some difficulty breathing.

We like to use a stiff, solid-braid check cord that is comfortable in the hand. If the rope is stiff, it is

easier to manipulate. You will find that a stiff cord is easier to keep out from underneath the dog, and easier to flip over his back when changing directions. Our check cords have solid bronze snaps that connect to the collar, and these snaps have a swivel to keep the check cord from twisting and becoming difficult to manage.

Begin the process of teaching a dog to check-cord by maintaining the behavioral expectations that you have put in place for all other exercises with your dog. Approach your dog with a calm demeanor, have him stand calmly while you snap the check cord into his collar (if he bounces around, stand up and wait for him to settle again). As you practice this routine every day, the dog will begin settling on his own quickly.

Once you have the check cord snapped to the collar and are ready to go, give your dog a soft touch on the top of the head to release him. We will begin developing this cue to release during the first portion of the Foundation training. This cue can be used any time you want send the dog forward quickly with confidence.

After the release, move off in the same direction as your dog and allow him to extend all the way to the end of the check cord. As he comes to the end of the check cord, change the direction you are walking and cue to have the dog turn with you on an angle that is 60 degrees opposite, and walk in that direction. In this way, you can begin to quarter your dog using a zig-zag pattern, not so much ensuring a consistent pattern, but rather ensuring that your dog note the cue and follow your indicated direction while staying in front. Cue the dog to turn when he is at 10 o'clock and 2 o'clock in relation to your body, as this will ensure that your dog is working ahead of you.

There are a few concepts to remain aware of while check-cording. First, make sure that you continue to change direction as you work down the field. There are multiple reasons for changing direction, the first being that your goal is to teach your dog to turn on a cue on the neck. The second reason for changing direction frequently actually takes into account your own self-preservation, as a

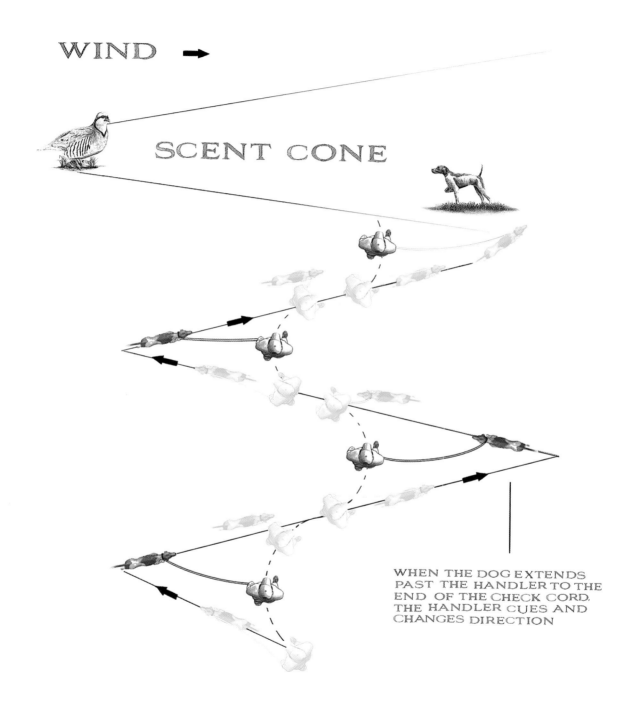

WIND →

SCENT CONE

WHEN THE DOG EXTENDS
PAST THE HANDLER TO THE
END OF THE CHECK CORD,
THE HANDLER CUES AND
CHANGES DIRECTION

Check-cording allows you the opportunity to begin teaching your dog to stay toward the front and change directions as you do. This is the onset of developing a dog that goes with you in the field.

POINTS TO CHECK-CORDING YOUR DOG EFFECTIVELY

> First, do not allow your dog to circle behind you while check-cording. If you do, he will learn that it is okay to circle you in the field, effectively working back behind you in a way that is inefficient. A dog should always hunt in front of the handler.

> Remember that check-cording is a dynamic exercise. Continually work up and down your check cord to remove the bulk of the slack between you and your dog. As your dog approaches the end of the check cord, turn him with a cue and redirect him so that he goes with you and to the front, then let the dog work out to the end of the cord again. While check-cording, the rope should continually be moving in your hands.

> Keep the check cord out from underneath your dog. The point of contact that you are working is the neck. If the check cord gets under your dog or around a leg, the cue is muddied and unclear. If the rope does get underneath your dog's leg, try to sort it without too much fuss and continue on. Keeping slack out of your rope will help in keeping the rope from getting tangled with your dog. With practice, you can learn how to give the rope a slight flick with your wrist to roll it over the dog's back smoothly as he changes direction.

> When working up and down the cord, allow the tail end of the check cord to drag on the ground. Don't worry about coiling or otherwise managing the dragging end. This will help to keep you from getting tangled up in the tail of the rope.

> Be an indicator for your dog. Always move your body in the direction that you would like your dog to go. If you want your dog to move a certain direction, you should be moving that direction as well. Give your dog clear leadership. Never stand in one spot and expect your dog to keep moving.

> If check-cording feels like work, you are probably doing it right! Maintaining contact with the dog, covering ground, and providing a solid number of cues and turns will keep you moving and on your toes.

> Remember that check-cording is the progression to going with you in the field.

big dog who uses his weight will almost always go into a roading mindset if the handler bobs along behind him like a dead weight. When the handler simply follows in-line, the dog leans into the weight, pulling like he has a harness on. When this pattern plays out, by the end of the workout both dog and handler are physically spent. Nothing is gained from such a workout except perhaps physical exercise. By changing direction consistently during check-cording sessions, a handler will also gain better control of the animal, teaching the dog to change direction on cue.

TEACHING A RECALL

While working with the check cord, we can begin to introduce a cue for recall. With your dog moving directly away from you, give a cue on your dog's neck using the check cord. Your goal is to have the dog turn around 180 degrees and come straight back to you, stand calmly in front of you with his attention focused on you, and remain receptive and ready to do what you ask next.

Your cue should be just strong enough to gain the dog's attention and get his focus on you. If you cue and the dog's body does not change at all, the cue was probably unclear or not strong enough for him to be aware of. Remember: *The level of distraction always determines the level of intensity required for an effective cue.* Always begin new obedience exercises in controlled environments where there are not many distractions (i.e. inside the house or in the backyard) and introduce new exercises in a manner that sets your dog up for success.

If your dog deviates from a straight path to you during a recall, simply cue again to gain his focus, getting him to come straight in to you. As you work on the recall, also think about how you would like your dog to deliver a bird to you down the road. The behavior you see on the recall will be the same on the retrieve—after all a retrieve is simply a recall with the dog carrying something in his mouth. For this reason, we like dogs to come straight in and stand in front of the trainer, looking up at him or her in a receptive manner. Such behavior develops an easy delivery on the retrieve.

When cueing your dog to come to you, it may be helpful to give him a visual or audible target. Some of the visual aids we use to encourage a good recall include kneeling down in an inviting manner, snapping your fingers, or clapping your hands together to provide an audilble target. This will help keep your dog's attention directly on you as he comes in. Keep in mind that you are not physically pulling a dog to you on a rope, you are cueing a dog to make the decision to come to you. Look for the moment that the dog's body language changes as he makes that decision. Often a dog's body language will change instantly as he makes the decision. Usually they will look directly at you when they have decided to comply.

Generally speaking, a dog moves in the direction that he is looking. Pay close attention to this while working to build a good recall. If your dog begins to come to you and then looks away, re-cue him to redirect him to you. You want to the dog to begin coming back to you on a straight path without diverging.

Be an indicator for your dog. Always move your body in the direction that you would like your dog to go. If you want your dog to move a certain direction, you should be moving that direction as well. Give your dog clear leadership. Never stand in one spot and expect your dog to keep moving.

After your dog has come to you, take the opportunity to rub on him and build up your connection with him. That said, keep in mind how your behavior will impact his behavior; giving your dog a

calm rub down will probably reduce any stress in his mind, benefit his general state of mind, and encourage him to stand calmly by you. An excited, energetic, exuberant touch and voice is likely to make him bounce around, get a case of "happy feet," and bounce out of shape, requiring a new correction from you to get him to stand calmly. Your demeanor can either set your dog up for success or set him up for failure. Remember, you are always teaching behavior and developing habits with your dog. Make sure that the behavior that is modeled and encouraged is indeed the behavior that you want to see every time, whether your dog is working in the field or living in the home.

Keep in mind that the most important part of this exercise is to teach the dog to make his own decision to come to you, not to physically pull him toward you. If your cue is correct, it may take a second for the dog to process the situation and make the decision to come to you. That is fine. With repetition, he will move past needing that time to consider his options and instead will come straight in. The goal of this exercise is to create an ingrained response.

FIELD WORK: SETTING UP THE WORKOUT
As you set out to plant your training birds in the field, you must constantly analyze the layout and the factors that will impact your dog's progress. First, consider the wind and airflow; you always want to cast your dog across the scent cone so that he can clearly telegraph when he has caught scent of the bird. To do so, you need to know the wind conditions and how the air is moving in the location where you intend to plant the bird.

The bird's scent cone is just that—namely the cone of scent that comes off the bird, getting wider and less concentrated as the distance from the bird increases. It will emanate from the bird and spread downwind from there, so if the bird is planted in thick vegetation on a rise in the terrain or even downwind of a large structure, scenting conditions will be impacted. Be aware of what the airflow is doing at the particular spot where you plant a bird.

Another factor to consider in choosing a location to plant your bird is the potential lesson communicated to your dog about likely cover. You will want your dog to associate finding birds with areas that would be considered "birdy." A "birdy" spot typically has some identifiable characteristic, perhaps a weedy or brushy hedgerow or a clump of cover. By planting your birds in places similar to those in which you might naturally find birds, you will teach your dog to gravitate to likely cover. This will help him become a more proficient bird finder when he is eventually working an area on his own, without the guidance of a check cord. Be certain, however, not to plant a bird in same structure, or under the same bush, every workout. Change your planting sites so that your dog is not running the course by memory without actually hunting.

Be sure to plant a bird where the dog will not be able to see it. If necessary, bend down and look at the location from your dog's perspective; if you determine that a dog can see through the vegetation to the bird, replant the bird somewhere else, or move some vegetation to build a visual screen on the downwind side of the planted bird. You must teach your dog to locate birds by scent, not by sight.

A quick note here about visual dogs: In today's society, dogs are asked to live in a highly visual world. If they are in a backyard, there is likely little game that they can pursue using their nose. That said, well within sight there may be a squirrel running up the power feed to the house or a bird feeder crowded with songbirds. Songbirds and squirrels are commonly the only game that a dog gets to see on a day-to-day basis, and these daily exposures teach suburban dogs to hunt with their eyes, rather than their noses. This takes some retraining when those dogs begin working birds in the field. As long as visual reliance is not too deeply ingrained in a dog's behavior, matters usually work themselves out naturally, provided the dog's success in locating game by scent outweighs his success in locating visual targets.

Once the field is set with a few pigeons, be sure to step back and mentally note the exact location of each planted bird. It is imperative that you know the exact location of your planted birds in the early stages of training, so that you can set your dog up for success in the lesson. A guess at where the bird is will lead to sloppy bird work, because you will not be able to successfully present bird scent to your dog in a manner that ensures an abrupt intersection with the scent cone and an intense point.

THE BIRD WORKOUT

Start your bird workouts with your dog on a tie-out, in a dog box, or in a crate. As mentioned above, tie-outs serve as a safe place to station your dog while you are getting the field set, but just as importantly the tie-out acts as a classroom. When canine students get to the classroom, they learn how to patiently wait their turn and to "clock in" at the correct time. Begin your session by approaching your dog. As you approach, make a point to be neutral in both demeanor and emotion. Remember, dogs are champions at reading body language and at assessing our emotions, so the less emotion you exude, the more relaxed your dog will be. In the first few days of this stage of training, your dog will bounce around significantly at your approach. Your dog will be happy to have your attention and will be eager to go looking for birds. You need to require your dog to "present" himself and stand calmly, and by waiting until he is through his excitement, you can start building behavior.

To reiterate, if you approach your dog on the tie-out, keep him on the side that you will heel him from. Only once a dog stands still should you reach down and calmly rub on him. Should he move again, simply stand up and go neutral. After you dog is standing calmly, reach down, rub his back and withers, then place your equipment on him. At this stage in training, your equipment consists of a 20-foot check cord that you can snap to the D-ring on the dog's collar. In later training stages the required equipment will be a training collar. Once your dog is on the check cord, unsnap him from the tie-out lead and anticipate that he will likely move forward when he hears or feels the snap release. If necessary, cue the dog with the check cord to set him back into his original position. As soon as the dog moves back, give him a loose lead and help him

make the decision to stand at heel on a loose lead.*

Once your dog has stood calmly by your side for a few seconds, touch him on the head to release him. Work him out to the bird field on the check cord in a short, quartering progression. Check-cording out to the bird field allows you to start teaching a dog to go with you at a short distance and reinforces the idea that the dog should turn when cued. Bear in mind that check-cording is a dynamic exercise with the goal of having the dog work ahead of you in a zig-zag pattern, turning when cued in order to pass in front of you. As you and your dog zig-zag your way into the field, you should constantly work up and down the length of the check cord, keeping the slack out of the system as the dog comes closer and goes out again. This process replicates what was exercised in the yard without birds, but in this case, you will be working your dog in such a direction that he will sharply intersect the scent cone of the planted bird.

THE APPROACH TO THE BIRD

It is imperative that you know exactly where the bird is, where the scent cone is, and how to approach the scent cone for maximum reward. The goal here is to introduce your dog to the scent of a bird in an orientation that keeps your dog a number of feet away from the bird, but high enough up the scent cone that the scent is strong. In an ideal situation, your dog will cross the scent cone and immediately telegraph that he has caught scent, thus allowing you to stop him on point.

To successfully present a bird encounter to a dog in a consistent manner takes practice. Pay attention to the scenting conditions and how your dog reacts when he does not experience a proper presentation to the bird, as your dog will be your best indicator of effectiveness. There are some behaviors that telegraph a poor presentation: If your dog is not able to smell the bird until he is practically on top of it, he will not snap to an intense, classic point. To the contrary, a dog that gets too close will tend to get low or crouch on the front end and try to pounce in to catch the bird. If your dog is brought into a bird too far down the scent cone and therefore in a spot

Set your dog up for success by check-cording him into the scent cone so that you know when he catches scent by the immediate change in his body language.

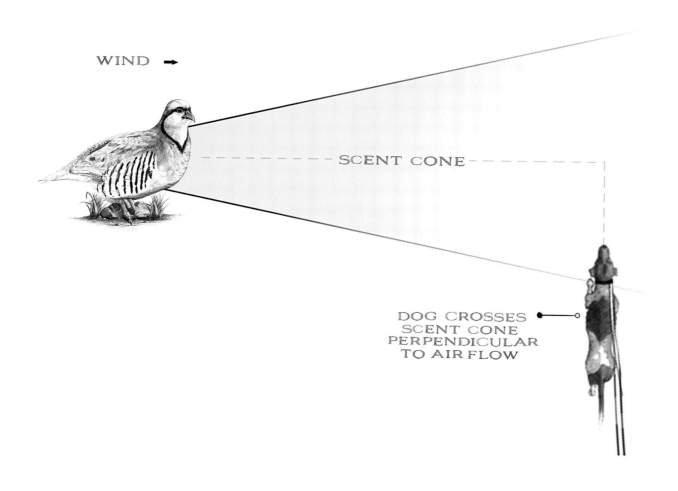

WIND ➡

SCENT CONE

DOG CROSSES
SCENT CONE
PERPENDICULAR
TO AIR FLOW

//

At the risk of over-emphasizing this point, it is noteworthy that humans often try to gain control of an animal by physically manipulating its movement. In training a dog, that often means that a handler attempts to use the check cord to manually hold the dog in place. Since the dog weighs less than a human, this approach pretty much works. However, The Smith Training Method hinges upon the philosophy that a trainer must help the dog make the decision to do what the trainer wishes, without physically forcing the dog to do the trainer's will. Keep this in mind as you work your dog. Dogs have to be given the leeway to make infractions, so that they can learn the difference between a good decision and an erroneous one.

//

where the scent cone is diffuse and weak, your dog will most likely catch a light whiff of the bird and road in, or lean into the cord and work straight up the cone forcefully. This scenario teaches the dog to road in on scent rather than working scent and stopping when he hits scent.

Determining the perfect location to cross the scent cone and thereby present your dog to maximum bird scent can be challenging. It varies significantly according to the wind, humidity, and the focus of your dog. If all conditions are favorable—there is a slight breeze, it is not too humid and not too dry, and your dog is focused—your dog can generally scent a well-concealed pigeon from 5 to15 feet away. As with most matters dealing with animals, there are exceptions to that rule! As a trainer, you will have to develop a feel for conditions and the dog's proficiency through repetition, striving all the while to make a better bird presentation every time.

It is important that you shorten up your rope as you approach the bird location so that you have added control of your dog. Simultaneously, you must prepare to cast the dog across the scent cone and back out the other side if he does not catch scent. If he does pass through the scent cone without recognizing the scent, cast him out a short distance then bring him back across the scent cone a little closer to the bird. In this manner you will work up the intensity of the scent cone until your dog telegraphs that he does indeed detect scent.

Make sure that you continue to walk with your dog, never standing still. It is a human tendency to stand in the scent cone and to cast the dog from side to side by using arm motions. This typically leads to dogs aimlessly milling around and going behind the handler. When points are established this way, they are typically sloppy and lacking in style. It is much cleaner to cast the dog through the scent cone and not change your pace until you are past the cone, and then cue your dog back into the scent cone. Try to never indicate to your dog that there is a bird nearby by changing your pace or demeanor. Allow him to locate the bird as naturally as possible.

Once your dog indicates that he has smelled the bird, stop him with the check cord. With repetition, you will begin to gain a feel for the animal. With time, you will know whether you must continue to physically hold your dog still with the rope or if you can allow a little slack in the rope, building on the dog's pointing ability without your interference. If a dog will stand staunchly on point this way, give him a few seconds, allow him to take it all in and build that desirable behavior.

As you prepare to flush the bird, quietly work up the rope toward your dog. As you get close to your dog, kneel down and place one hand in his collar and one arm around his flank. The knee closest to your dog will be on the ground and the opposite leg firmly braced in a kneeling position to help hold your dog if he begins to move around. The goal here is to essentially serve as an "invisible force" holding your dog still in the exact place where he established point. You do not want to speak, move quickly, pet your dog, or give him any cause to move or distraction. You do not want to break your dog's focus and thereby intensity on bird scent. You simply want to hold your dog still through the flush.

TIPS:

> Handlers often pick up their dog and adjust the dog's location to match where the handler kneeled down. This happens most frequently when that handler kneels down too far away from a dog, and instead of the handler adjusting his or her position, the dog is pulled backward. Try instead to consciously kneel directly beside your dog and adjust your body to match his.

> Don't allow the dog to get too close to the bird before establishing point. Bringing a dog closer than 3 feet from the bird is likely to create a dog that pulls in with a low-set body and a desire to flush, and it promotes a flushing mindset rather than creating a staunch point.

> Refrain from petting, talking to, or styling your dog while he is on point. This serves as a distrac-

Kneel beside your dog and gently hold him with one hand in the collar and one are around the flank as the bird is flushed.

tion for your dog and can cause him to have less intensity on point.

When you are in position, with one hand in the dog's collar, the other arm around the flank, and a firm hold on the dog, it is time to flush the bird. Whether using a tip-up, a mechanical release, or an electronic launcher—it is beneficial to have someone else act as a flusher. Try to keep the flush as similar to a flush on a hunt as possible, with everyone present striving to keep the environment natural, without much talking or hoopla.

During the early portion of the Foundation Level of training, if your dog has a high prey drive and previous experience on birds during your puppy development, you can allow your dog to break on the flush and to chase so that you can properly introduce the gun. Once you are comfortable that gunfire has been successfully introduced, you can begin either holding you dog steady through the gun report or allow him to break on the report—more on gun introduction in a moment.

is using his nose to locate game, and has exhibited a strong chase when the bird flies—he is ready to be properly introduced to the gun. We treat every dog that comes through our program as if he might have a gun-shyness issue, and we don't ever shoot just to see if a dog has a problem with gunfire. We use desensitization and prey drive to ensure that gun-shyness is not a problem during training. As a result, we rarely have any issues with the gun.

The day you decide your dog is ready to be introduced to the gun, set your normal field for a bird workout. When you take your dog out to the field, be sure you have a bag of extra birds to flush if they are needed, and, of course, bring a blank pistol with as light of a load as possible. Allow your dog to point and then flush the planted bird as usual. As your dog is chasing hard after the bird and is a distance away from you, keep your eyes on your dog and fire the pistol once. If your dog continues to run without changing anything in his pace or body language, proceed to the next bird as normal and perform the same routine. If, however, the dog turns to you or stops chasing the flying bird altogether, immediately pull a bird out of your bag and fly it toward the dog's direction to incite his prey drive to pursue that bird. The focus here is to turn any potential negative association with the report of the gun into a positive association, as the dog gains another bird to pursue.

Repetition, desensitization, and positive association are key in getting a dog over any sound issues. Nonetheless, be aware that a dog that has previously exhibited sound sensitivity will most likely always be somewhat sound-sensitive. Typically, a dog is not magically cured of sound sensitivity, unless there is an underlying issue that is addressed, thereby alleviating the sound issue. By

HELPFUL INDICATORS OF THE ZONES OF BIRD APPROACH

> **Too close:** shown by flagging, low in the front end, or laying down

> **Too far:** flagging and general lack of intensity

> **Just right:** high on both ends, good intensity; typically 5 to 8 feet away from the bird is a sweet spot

GUN INTRODUCTION

Once your dog's prey drive is at a pinnacle, his focus is on birds as soon as he gets to the field, he

using a dog's high prey drive and desensitizing him to the sound of the gun, you can get a sound-sensitive dog through training and successfully use him in the field. However, if there is a period of time during which that dog is not exposed to gunfire and birds, he will most likely revert back to being sensitive to loud sounds. If a sound-sensitive dog is laid off during the summer, be aware that when the season starts back up, he will need to undergo some desensitization training to ease him back into peak performance. Do not take that laid-off dog out on opening day of pheasant season and shoot over him as if he never had any issue, as you can create huge problems by doing so. A sound-sensitive dog needs to be reintroduced to sound incrementally in a controlled environment and desensitized again. Sound sensitivity is an issue that a handler will need to be aware of and be prepared to manage for the rest of the dog's life. If managed properly, however, it will not mean the end of a dog's hunting career.

If introduced correctly to gunfire, most dogs will have no sound-sensitivity issues. Their training can progress forward easily. Slowly increase the size and intensity of the starter pistol or shotgun load and decrease the distance of the shot until both handler and dog are comfortable with scenarios that might occur in a natural hunting episode.

BACKING: STAND STILL

If you ever plan to run your trained dog with a bracemate or a group, you will want to teach your dog to back, or honor, another dog's point. Backing is simply the act of a dog acknowledging that another dog is on point and stopping to honor that point as soon as the trailing dog sees the pointing dog. Backing ensures that a trailing dog will not steal another dog's point, flush a pointed bird, or otherwise create an uncontrollable environment when a bird is pointed. Steady backing also ensures safety in the field, as backing dogs are static and stationary, allowing shooters a clear sense of their location.

Lessons in backing are sight-oriented drills that can be introduced during the check-cording drills in the bird field. To accomplish these drills initially, you will need to have enough help and enough dogs to run two in tandem, or you must have a remote backing dog or plywood cutout of a dog on point.

When running a brace of dogs in a backing drill, have the first dog proceed to the field for bird work. Allowing a bit of distance, say 30 to 50 yards of separation, the second handler can check-cord dog #2 out into the field behind the first dog. When the first dog crosses scent and goes on point, the second handler can check-cord his dog into such a position that his dog can see the pointing dog. As soon as the backing dog sees the pointing dog, he should be stopped with the check cord. It does not really matter how far away the backing dog is from the pointing dog when he is stopped; this is a strictly visual exercise, and all that the handler should be looking for is for his dog to see the other dog on point. Once the handler has stopped the backing dog, he or she should work up the rope to the dog, kneel, and hold the dog through the flush, just the same as the pointing dog. Once the bird is flushed, release both dogs with a touch on the head, and check-cord on into a succession of birds. We like to alternate and make sure each dog in a brace gets both a point and a back during any single workout.

Training teaches your dog to make good decisions on his own, such as heeling on a loose lead rather than physically being held close by his handler.

OBEDIENCE WORKOUTS

//

HEELING ON A LOOSE LEAD

Heeling is the onset of having a dog *go with you*. This is simply the process of having your dog walk calmly at your side on a loose lead, with the dog on the shooter's left for a right-handed gunner and the inverse for a left-handed gunner. A heeling dog should not lag behind or pull ahead, should not veer off or lean into you, and should generally remain mindful of your cadence as you move. Heeling also helps a dog become settled, encourages him to join up with and listen closely to the cues of his handler, and step into a mannerly state of mind. By beginning to teach dogs to pay attention to your body and go with you in the controlled environment, you can set them up for successfully learning to go with you at a distance in the field.

Heeling has a lot of practical physical benefit for both dog and handler as well. A dog that is constantly pulling on a leash is unpleasant to be with and can be unwieldy for a handler who cannot physically manage a pulling dog. Similarly, pulling on a lead can damage the dog's throat, causing scar tissue to build up and thereby restricting airflow. If a dog gets in a bind in the field (think: overheated, porcupine incident, cut, pulled muscle, etc.), heeling is a good way to settle the dog and manage the stressing event, as it allows blood pressure and temperature to drop while also calming the dog's mind as you make your way back to the truck.

We have been called on to rely on our heeling as a tool in the field innumerable times, occasionally under circumstances that could have become quite challenging had the dog not been capable of settling and going with us on a loose lead. One notable incident took place while we were working dogs on a hot Montana day in September. We had run a set of four dogs about a half-mile through the prairie to a shelter belt that we knew was shady and thick with resting birds. We each took a brace of two dogs and went in separate directions, meeting up when we had each gotten sufficient bird work with the particular brace we were running. By the time we had achieved the contacts we wanted, all four dogs were quite hot and our water supply was almost fully depleted. It was obvious to us that a couple of the dogs would risk overheating if we allowed them to free-run back to the vehicle. Due to the discipline that we'd instilled in the dog's basic training, we were able salvage the potentially dangerous situation and confidently place the two braces of dogs on an off-lead heel back to the truck in a calm, relaxed mindset. Each of us walked with two dogs paired by our side across the pasture. This controlled walk allowed all four dogs to cool down before we even reached the additional water and shade that the truck provided. All dogs arrived back at the truck with closed mouths and relaxed minds, in good shape to digest a training session that could otherwise have proven quite unproductive or even dangerous. Had they either pulled on a lead or been allowed to run all the way back to the truck, those dogs would have arrived in a dangerously hot physical state. We can duplicate experiences like that all over the country; one could simply substitute these overheated dogs with dogs with fence lacerations to porcupine and

//

ABOVE: The Command Lead should be placed just behind the dog's ears with enough slack that the dog is comfortable but cannot easily slip out of the rope.

javelina encounters. There is significant value in having a dog be able to heel calmly on cue.

TEACHING YOUR DOG TO HEEL WITH THE COMMAND LEAD

Each training element begins with teaching a point of contact mechanically with a rope and then later utilizing that point of contact to transition to remote cues of the collar. To begin teaching dogs to heel, we rely on what is known as a Command Lead. The Command Lead is a stiff, 6-foot rope made of a two-strand, wax-coated nylon that creates a simple loop with a hondo, much like a cowboy's lariat. This tool was developed by Delmar Smith, and it was given its original name "The Wonder Lead" by a talented trainer named Ed Rader. Ed was often quoted as saying of the lead, "You'll wonder how you ever got along without it." The name stuck for decades, and it is often still referred to as "The Wonder Lead." Whichever name you prefer to use, this lead is an invaluable tool to teach a dog about cues to the neck, to teach heeling, and to teach a dog to properly join up with you.

The Smith family has had the Command Lead manufactured for decades, and as trainers, we have used it successfully on a wide array of canine personalities. Simply put, there has yet to be a dog that we couldn't teach to heel with the Command Lead. Its efficiency is in part due to the stiffness of the material, which enables the loop that goes around the dog's neck to stay as open as possible, as if it is spring-loaded to release. There is a rubber grommet or stopper that can be slid into place to customize the size of the loop around the dog's neck, and we recommend positioning the stopper in such a way that the circumference of the loop, once it is on the dog's neck, is just small enough that the dog cannot easily duck out of it. Due to the spring-like nature of the material, the loop will stay as open as the stopper will allow, and after a cue is given, the Command Lead automatically springs the loop back open, releasing pressure and thereby releasing the cue. The Command Lead affords a distinct cue and release every time, with the release being the key—as the dog learns the

A good example of heeling on a loose lead

most from the release, not the cue itself.

When teaching a dog to heel, you will want the dog's head to be even with your leg. This becomes the "sweet spot," and a dog positioned anywhere else is not properly heeling. A dog that understands the concept of heeling will walk with you no matter where you go and no matter the speed you walk or run. As your dog gains proficiency during practice sessions, you should change speed regularly and challenge him periodically with new situations, obstacles, and distractions. Many dogs will surprise you with how well they can heel in a variety of situations!

From a trainer's standpoint, the most challenging aspect of effectively teaching your dog to heel is getting over a common human tendency. When you ask your dog to heel, it is critical that you give your dog a loose lead. It is human nature to try to make a dog walk at heel by holding that dog on a tight lead, physically holding the dog where the handler decides the dog should be. It is our comfort zone to physically hold and control the dog on a lead. It is

very difficult for people to give an animal his head, as we tend to feel that in doing so, we relinquish control of the situation. However, when you heel a dog on a loose lead you teach him to make the decision on his own to walk with you. Your dog can choose to do as asked rather than being physically held back on a rope. If your dog walks beside you on a tight lead, he isn't heeling—he is just being physically held back. In order to learn to heel properly, a dog simply has to be given a loose lead and allowed the opportunity to comply on his own.

To use the Command Lead to teach heeling, first create a big loop and slip it over the dog's head. The hondo, or fixed loop through which the rope slips, should be on the side closest to you. Bring the stopper down to a point that keeps the loop with an inch or two of slack around the dog's neck. The rope should be placed just behind the dog's ears, high up on his neck. The reasoning for this positioning is the same with just about any animal: The lower the rope is positioned on the neck, the less control the handler has of the animal. A rope high on the neck of an animal will control his head, which in turn controls his body. A rope that is positioned low on a dog's neck encourages him to push against the pressure, acting more like a harness. Be certain when bringing the lead over the dog's head, that the opening in the lead loop is large enough to pass over his head and give him plenty of space to not feel like he should move his head to avoid the close object. The dog has to feel comfortable with the loop passing over his head. A small loop may intimidate a dog, tending to make him act "head-shy" as the object moves close past his eyes and ears. Make a nice open loop and pass it over the dog's head without it touching the dog at all. Once the loop is on the dog's neck, readjust the sizing to fit properly.

Once the lead is on the dog, stand and let the dog settle, then start moving forward with the dog in a heeling position. Early on, the tendency will be for the dog to either lag behind or pull ahead, and for the handler to keep tension on the lead, as noted above. Remember that you can always cue to correct, but if you maintain a tight lead you will neither have the slack that allows your dog to recognize the area where he should be walking, nor the slack to create a cue and release that actually teaches a lesson. A loose lead means that there is no direct pressure on the dog's neck as he walks at heel. When using the Command Lead, a sufficiently loose lead looks like a bow, or sag of slack, between the handler's hand and the dog's neck. A good rule of thumb is to add 6 inches of slack beyond what you feel comfortable with. If a cue is required, be sure to give back the slack and allow the release to take place.

When you teach any lesson on a lead or check cord, think of the rope as a direct line of communication between you and your dog. Picture yourself communicating with your dog through Morse code that is transmitted through the lead. Each time your lead has tension in it, you are sending a code to your dog. If the codes are not clear, the message you send to your dog will be confusing to him. Steady tension sounds like muffled static to your dog, rather than a clear and concise series of directives. Under steady tension, your dog will either become confused or simply decide that your cues do not mean anything, and he will typically revert to the default mode of pulling against the lead.

Begin your heeling lesson by attaching the Command Lead as instructed above and positioning the dog beside your leg, with the dog on your left side if you shoot right-handed and the dog on your right side if you shoot left-handed. Move forward with a loose lead and a clear, steady pace in a straight direction.

If your dog forges ahead, don't just pull him back. Instead, turn 180 degrees and walk with purpose in the opposite direction, cueing with a short tug on the lead and immediately giving slack after the cue when the dog complies and turns to go with you. By turning 180 degrees away from your dog, you are, in part, allowing the momentum of your dog to determine the strength of the cue, while also teaching the dog to pay attention to where you are and not assume that you'll follow along behind him.

If your dog lags behind, give a quick series of cues—cue, cue, cue—until he catches up. As you do this, maintain your speed. It is human nature for people to slow down in response to their dog slowing his pace. To help your dog, you should instead take a leadership role, maintain your pace, and walk with confidence while cueing your dog to come with you. As he catches up, be sure the lead is slack again.

If your dog curls in to your body, make a sharp 90-degree turn into your dog and bump him on his shoulder with your off-side knee as if you were walking through him. Don't let his being in the way dissuade you from taking that new line. It is his responsibility to respect your personal space as you walk toward him and yield to you by sliding back into position. Be aware that it is typical for people to do more turns away from their dog than it is for them to practice repeated turns into a dog. This consistent turn-away tends to cause a dog to walk at an angle, almost as if he has already begun the turn. By being aware of your natural human tendency to turn away and by recognizing the resulting behavior in your dog, you can quickly address the issue by making more turns into your dog. This exercise will bring your dog back into position and into line with

Heeling sessions are a great time to teach a young dog about cues on the neck. Always move in the opposite direction that the dog wants to move, giving a short cue and release to get the dog to come with you.

Do the opposite of what your dog does. If your dog forges ahead, as Grace does here, turn the opposite direction and cue your dog to go with you.

the direction that you are walking. Owing to this natural human inclination to turn away from a dog that is slightly ahead and in the human's way, we have instructed a number of our apprentices to take a certain dog from the tie-out to the kennel using only turns into the dog. This exercise of making only left-handed turns is harder than you'd think, but it helps to retrain any tendency to turn away from a dog!

The general rule of heeling is to do the opposite of what your dog does. Work into him or away from him to teach the desired behavior. Vary your speed, feel free to start and stop, and keep things calm and clear.

There is no need to give a command verbally at this point as the expectation will become that whenever the dog is on a lead at your side, he should heel like a gentleman and follow your lead. We will introduce the verbal cue only once he is heeling perfectly, and then the established perfect behavior is labeled "Heel."

Initially, you will find yourself making significant direction changes in response to big move-

ABOVE: To correct your dog's positioning, do the opposite. If your dog turns right (into your space), make a left-hand turn (into your dog's space) to correct your dog's positioning.

ments from your dog. As your dog begins to pay more attention to you, learning to assess your movements and adjust his movements accordingly, your cues and corrections will get smaller and subtler. Eventually, just the slightest cue will serve as a correction to get your dog back into heeling position. As your dog begins to gain an understanding of what you are asking, be aware of your tendency to want to micromanage—allow your dog to be successful as he gains an understanding of how to heel. As he gains proficiency, you will have the chance to fine-tune his position and be exacting in your behavioral requirements. Read your animal and don't put undue stress on him by being overly strict during the first couple of sessions. Generally speaking, it may take half a dozen sessions to get your dog heeling perfectly. Go at his pace.

If you realize that your dog is pushing against

you as you walk, there are a few ways to correct. First, as with any behavior, consider the reasoning behind your dog's action. Is he leaning in because he is trying to take control of the situation and stop you from moving? Is he feeling stress? Is he simply not paying attention, using physical contact as a means of knowing where you are without having to look at you? If you decide that your dog is trying to assert an alpha position and take control of the situation, just turn into him and walk with purpose—he will quickly learn to give to your personal space. If you decide your dog is feeling stress, pick your head up and relax your shoulder, helping to take pressure off of him, and walk somewhere in a straight line with purpose, making as few cues as possible and keeping the cues as light as possible. Allow him time to get in stride with you and relax. Sometimes dogs, just like people, just need a chance to clear their head and "get in the groove." If you decide he is pushing against you because he is simply not paying attention, you can flip the orientation of the Command Lead loop as it is placed over his head. Animals naturally move away from pressure, and by moving the hondo from the outside of the neck to the inside of the neck, the cue will cause your dog to want to move out slightly each time he feels pressure, thereby putting him in the proper position.

We generally hold the Command Lead between two fingers when we are cueing dogs. This allows us to be precise in our cue and subsequent release. The goal is to make lighter and lighter cues with each session until you and your dog are synchronized as you walk together and no cues from the Command Lead are necessary.

As your dog gains proficiency, be sure to pick your head up and look where you are going. Use this opportunity to simply go for a stroll with your dog. As handlers, we don't want to become the boss that is always looking over a shoulder and micromanaging. Give the dog the freedom to make some infractions and simply correct them when they arise. Other than that, try to create a relaxed, comfortable working environment for your dog.

Keep your heeling exercises short. Fifteen minutes per session is plenty. Your dog can learn a lot in a short, focused workout. You can also do multiple short sessions in a day.

THE WHOA POST: TEACHING A CUE TO STAND STILL

Perhaps the fundamental descriptive behavior that distinguishes a bird dog is his ability to slam on the brakes, ceasing all motion when the scent of a bird is encountered. This ability to stop midstream is the defining trait of a bird dog—a trait we have bred and selected for over hundreds, if not thousands, of years. Rarely, though, does a dog have a perfect point and the ability to apply it right out of the gate. A good point is a behavior we shape, refine, and implement in such a way that it becomes second nature. There are many ways to teach a dog to stand still, but years and generations have led us to believe that the Whoa Post lessons represent the clearest and most efficient means of teaching a dog that a cue on the flank means stop and stand still. We have literally taught thousands of dogs to stand still on the Whoa Post.

The main purpose of the Whoa Post is for your dog to build an association with the cue on the flank to stop. You are developing a point of contact on the flank so that your dog will have a conditioned response to stop when cued. That is not to say that there aren't a multitude of behaviors that can be addressed on the Whoa Post and numerous benefits that come from the Whoa Post sessions; indeed, there are. However, don't lose sight of the fact that the simple goal of the Whoa Post is to teach a dog to stand still when cued.

To begin Whoa Post work, you will need to locate a purpose-specific training area. This can be any open area with enough space to check-cord your dog up to the post with a few turns. Ideally, you will want to choose an area with few distractions—neither near your bird pen nor in the same area in which you work your dog on birds during field exercises. A large backyard or mowed area works great for the Whoa Post sessions.

The Whoa Post itself can be a stake, tree, fence, or any stationary object to which you can securely

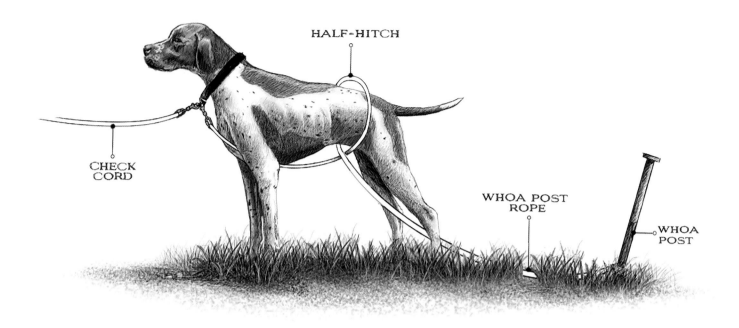

HALF-HITCH

CHECK
CORD

WHOA POST
ROPE

WHOA
POST

attach a soft rope that is approximately 20 feet long. Often in our training, we use a metal stake that we can drive into the soil deep enough to ensure that the dog cannot pull it loose. We drive the stake in to the ground and affix the rope to it. At the other end of the rope, we affix a snap and swivel that can be attached to the D-ring on the dog's leather collar. The rope used on a Whoa Post should be thick in diameter, approximately 1-inch thick, and soft to the touch. Do not use a check cord as a Whoa Post rope as it is too stiff and hard and will not be comfortable on your dog.

We begin our Whoa Post sessions by putting a check cord on our dog as he stands by our side. Give him a cue to release and then check-cord him into the training field to get him into a state of mind in which he is receptive to cues. Approach a Whoa Post with your dog on the check cord. Quarter your dog up to the post and along the Whoa Post rope that is laying on the ground. As you get near the end of the Whoa Post rope where the snap is connected, take the opportunity

to work on a recall—after all, a good trainer never passes up a teachable moment! Cue your dog to you, bringing him back along the path of the Whoa Post rope that is lying on the ground. As the recall is completed and your dog is standing calmly in front of you, he should be standing near the rope, just few feet away from the snap end of the Whoa Post rope. When your dog is standing still and the end of the Whoa Post rope is within your reach, reach down and run the snap end of the Whoa Post rope between your dog's back legs. Follow it up over his lower back and slip it underneath itself as it passes by the flank, essentially creating a half-hitch on the flank. Trace the snap end of the Whoa Post rope between the dog's front legs and snap it to the D-ring on his leather collar. When complete, you will have a rope that runs from the snap on the collar between the dog's front legs, around the dog's flank with a half-hitch, and between the dog's back legs to the stationary stake or post. There should be enough slack in the Whoa Post rope for the dog to take a

step before he feels a cue on the flank. Make sure there is not excessive slack in the Whoa Post rope between the dog's collar and the half-hitch on the flank. You want the rope to run along your dog's belly and not droop down below.

Have your dog stand calmly through this sequence. If he moves, make a leash correction with the check cord that is in your hand, wait to for him to settle, then finish hooking him up. It usually takes some work in the beginning to get your dog to stand still during this hooking-up process, but be consistent, and it will become easier for both you and the dog. Once the dog is set up with a half-hitch on the Whoa Post rope, slowly back away from him in-line with the Whoa Post rope. As you walk away, let the check cord feed through your hands, in order that you are able to back all the way to the end of the check cord. Typically, you will cue your dog when you are about 5 to 10 feet away from his head. If your dog moves before you are able to get much distance between you and him, be ready to take that opportunity to cue.

Set your dog up to move slowly into the cue without rushing forward. Rushing into a cue on the flank may overstimulate the dog. The goal here is to have the dog's forward movement be gently stopped by the rope, and to have the dog feel a snug cue on the flank.

Through this stage, concentrate on making fluid motions. As you move backwards while watching your dog, tighten your grip on the check cord and let your momentum bring the dog forward into the cue. Essentially, as you pull the dog gently away from the fixed point of the Whoa Post with the check cord, the cue will occur when your dog reaches the end of the Whoa Post rope and the half-hitch in the Whoa Post rope tightens. As the Whoa Post rope gets tight, the half-hitch makes contact with the dog's flank, a cue on the flank that establishes a point of contact to have the dog stand still.

Throughout this process, stand neutral and wait for your dog to acknowledge the cue. Do not talk to your dog, fidget, or move in any excessive manner. It is optimal for you to remain as neutral and calm as possible so that you do not interfere with your dog's ability to process the cue on his flank. Your

goal is to maintain just enough tension on the rope so that you can react in a timely manner if your dog tries to move at the end of the post. That being said, remaining still and calm can be a challenge. If you are nervous, angry, or simply not in a calm state of mind, your dog will know. The check cord clipped to your dog acts as a direct telegraph of emotion and energy, and your dog will remain very aware of your mindset through this exercise. If you are having a bad day and it is impeding your progress and impacting the dog, let the check cord touch the ground as you wait for an acknowledgment, as this will effectively break the line of communication between you and your dog. Removing your emotions will help the dog to think solely about the cue and react accurately to that alone.

After your dog has been cued by the rope around his flank, he should stand still until he is told with a cue on the head that he can move forward. If he chooses to move again before you have released him, simply re-cue with the Whoa Post rope. Once your dog has been cued to stand still, wait for him to mentally process the cue and give an acknowledgment. Sometimes this acknowledgment can occur almost immediately, while sometimes it may take a while. Have patience and let your dog sort out this new exercise on his own.

There are several possible indicators of processing that a dog will show you when he is mentally working through a new lesson. One of the most common indicators of processing occurs when your dog turns his head off to one side. Your dog might spend a moment looking intently at a branch swaying in the breeze, or he might even close his eyes, making you wonder if he is trying to take a nap. In fact, the dog is just trying to figure out the meaning of this apparatus on his flank and what the appropriate response is. Do not try to force your dog to maintain eye contact with you while he is going through this process—we have found that during this stage, asking a dog to look toward the trainer interferes with the natural process and puts undue stress on the dog. Allow your dog the time to mentally process what you are asking of him in this exercise. This may be the first time he has had

A licking of the lips or a yawn are the most
common types of acknowledgment

to stand entirely by himself and slowly figure something out, rather than simply reacting to a stimulus.

As soon as the dog works through the mental process and becomes more comfortable, he will give you an acknowledgment. That acknowledgment is your prompt to go to your dog, rub on him, and release him from the Whoa Post.

Noticing acknowledgment in this exercise requires close observation of subtle canine behaviors. A dog can communicate his acknowledgment by licking his lips, yawning, letting out a big sigh, repositioning his legs slightly to stand more squarely and comfortably, or even subtly softening his gaze.

Be patient with your dog and have faith in the system. Remember that the process of gaining acknowledgment at each post takes as long as it takes! Don't force it, and don't move forward too soon. Typically, the clearer you are with your cues, the quicker your dog will gain an understanding of what the Whoa Post aims to teach, and acknowledgments come more quickly with each session.

When you unhook your dog from the Whoa Post, you can make a clear release cue with a gentle touch on the head that tells your dog that he can move forward freely. This release is an important element of the training and should not be forgotten. If, in your dog's mind, it is clear that he gets cued to stand still and then cued to move on, it is simple to figure out how to be successful. Keep your dog learning by making the lessons black-and-white and easy to understand. Such clarity keeps confusion out of the equation. After you have given your dog a cue to release, check-cord him a little distance away from the Whoa Post so that he can loosen up and relax, then proceed to the next Whoa Post. Provide your dog with three Whoa Posts each training session.

THE THREE PHASES OF THE WHOA POST

There are three distinct phases in the Whoa Post drill, namely the Introductory Phase (typically 3 to 9 posts), the Association Phase (typically 20 to

In the Whoa Post sessions, a dog must be pulled to the end of the Whoa Post rope with a check cord. Once the cue on the flank is felt, the pull is released and the dog is allowed to process the lesson.

30 posts), and the Transition Phase (typically 3 to 9 posts). In the Introductory Phase, your primary goal is to simply introduce your dog to the Whoa Post and get him comfortable. This is likely to be the first time your dog has ever had a rope placed on his flank, and like the first time a collar was placed on his neck, the entire experience is probably going to feel odd to him. Use gentle cues to ease him into the exercise and allow him to process the fact that it is okay to have a rope around his flank.

The majority of dogs that have been well-socialized will accept this new apparatus easily. That said, some dogs may react strongly to it and may struggle to pull away from the apparatus or the check cord. Usually those dogs that struggle on the Whoa Post are dogs that are feeling mental stress for other reasons, have other issues that hamper their ability to be receptive to any type of training, or they are dogs that have deeply ingrained default behaviors that are an additional hurdle for them in training.

A dog that is under a significant amount of mental stress will likely interpret any new situation inaccurately, and the Whoa Post is no exception. If you notice that your dog is feeling stress when you begin the Whoa Post training, you can spend additional time addressing the underlying causes of that stress. Take some time to rub your dog's neck and back muscles to help eliminate excess stress from the body. It is imperative that your dog be in a positive state of mind when he begins any new course of training or experiences any new training tool, so that he can properly interpret what you are asking of him.

During the introduction of the Whoa Post, your dog may exhibit some default behaviors. A default behavior is a conditioned response that a dog has learned over the course of his lifetime. These are behaviors they have applied successfully and habitually through life.

RESHAPING DEFAULT BEHAVIORS
Typically, during Whoa Post sessions, the default behaviors that appear are sitting, laying on elbows, laying down completely, vocalizing, or flight responses. These behaviors predictably show themselves during the first few sessions on the Whoa Post.

Luckily, the Whoa Post session is an ideal place to start helping stressed dogs work through those undesirable behaviors, move beyond them, and become more healthy-minded animals. There are very few situations that you can set up that will create as perfectly controlled an environment as the Whoa Post. While working a dog on the Whoa Post, you will essentially be able to maintain physical control of him while also setting him up to successfully process issues he has never before been able to conquer on his own. As a tool, the Whoa Post allows you to help reshape negative behavior and build the new desired behavior of simply calmly standing still when cued on the flank.

The most common default behavior that shows up in response to the Whoa Post cue on the flank is sitting. Often, the first command that a young dog is taught is to sit. It is typically the only method an owner has of gaining control of an exuberant puppy, even if just for a moment. Generally speaking, sitting is a great discipline for any house dog to master, as it is an easy way for a dog to learn some manners. That said, pointing dogs provide an exception to this rule because the default behavior of sitting can transition into field and bird work. Sitting on scent does not impact a dog's ability to locate game, but it often impacts how the handler and hunter feel about the execution! We all tend to want that "classic point" and seeing a dog sit on point or during a back typically does not evoke the same feelings we are conditioned to feel.

The Whoa Post is a great opportunity to work through the sitting default. Your dog is in a completely controlled environment, and you can easily create a situation where your dog learns that the only way to be successful is to stand, not sit. Start this lesson in the Introductory Phase by first making sure that your dog successfully accepts the Whoa Post rope. Bring him gently to the end of the Whoa Post rope with the check cord to initiate a cue. From there, when your dog sits down, you will need to ask him to stand back up. To accomplish this on the Whoa Post, simply cue your dog from a 45-degree angle to bring him forward onto his feet. After the dog rises to his feet, simply give him slack

The main purpose of the Whoa Post is for your dog to build an association with the cue on the flank to stop. This will later transition to a low-level cue of the training collar, giving the handler the ability to confidently stop a dog at any time.

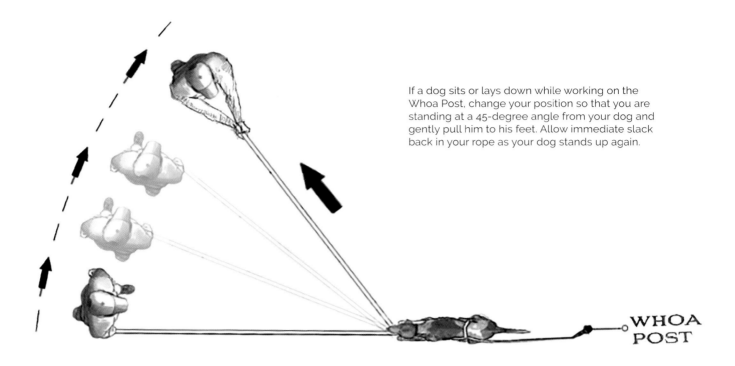

If a dog sits or lays down while working on the Whoa Post, change your position so that you are standing at a 45-degree angle from your dog and gently pull him to his feet. Allow immediate slack back in your rope as your dog stands up again.

WHOA POST

in the check cord and walk back so that the check cord is straight in line with the Whoa Post rope, and wait for an acknowledgment. Once you see the dog acknowledge, walk to him, unhook him from the Whoa Post rope, and touch his head to release.

The second most common default behavior seen during the Whoa Post sessions occurs when a dog lays down in response to stimuli. Dogs often pick up this passive-aggressive behavior at a young age when they are successful in making some intimidating, confusing, or adverse situation go away by simply laying down. The dog quickly learns that this is a way to successfully change the environment and make stressors stop. Again, the Whoa Post is a great opportunity to work through this behavior.

If your dog has lain down while on the Whoa Post, move over to create a 45-degree angle, which will help your dog be able to stand up on cue. Using a soft pull, try to gently roll your dog to his feet. It may take a few attempts to get your dog to successfully stand on his feet, depending on the level

of stress that your dog is feeling and his overall mental state. If he is feeling stress, take your time and accept small incremental successes. If your dog is laying down more as a default reaction with little or no emotion involved, you can require more rapid progress. Once your dog stands up, give him slack and a moment to relax and therefore be successful. After he stands up, line back up with the Whoa Post rope and wait for the acknowledgment before going to him to release.

A dog with a deeply ingrained flight response may fight the restriction of the Whoa Post rope. In today's society, our dogs are usually socialized enough that this flight response is not very common. However, should this happen, simply keep enough slack out of the check cord and Whoa Post rope to ensure that he does not get tangled up. It is your job as the trainer to safeguard the dog from getting himself in a bind. If your dog strongly resists the Whoa Post, he may end up lying down or rolling over. In that scenario, after the dog ceases fighting,

A dog may lay down or sit down as they work to decipher what you are trying to teach them on the Whoa Post. Gently and patiently work through these default behaviors while in the controlled environment of the Whoa Post so that you do not see them reappear in the bird field.

simply step off at an angle and gently bring him back to his feet as described previously. Once your dog is on his feet, line back up with the Whoa Post rope and wait for your dog's acknowledgment.

A dog that has any additional issues—poor socialization, poor understanding of any type of restriction from a rope, etc.—or default behaviors will exhibit more stress on the Whoa Post than the average dog. Keep this in mind as you work your dog. The first order of business will be to help your dog work through his mental and emotional baggage—teaching him a cue on the flank is only possible after that baggage has been effectively dealt with. Gently yet firmly guide your dog to success, go at his pace, and do not overstimulate him.

THE PROGRESSION OF THE WHOA POST

During the Introductory Phase of the Whoa Post, your goal is to concentrate simply on introducing your dog to the Whoa Post, ensuring that he is successful and maintains a receptive state of mind.

Practice effectively getting the dog onto the Whoa Post rope and gently bringing him forward just enough that he can feel the cue on his flank. A daily Whoa Post workout typically consists of three individual Whoa Posts, and this Introductory Phase generally lasts for three to nine posts achieved over one to three days. By the end of the third day, most dogs have accepted the Whoa Post and are in a receptive and teachable state of mind.

In the Association Phase of the Whoa Post, the exercise gets easier and more efficient. Again, check-cord your dog into the Whoa Post and snap the Whoa Post rope to the flat leather collar. Cue your dog to the end of the Whoa Post rope until tension is felt, then release the stimulation of the tightened half-hitch after approximately 1/2-second. Make sure this is a smooth cue-and-release motion and not a jerk of the rope. There needs to be just enough tension on the rope so that your dog feels a cue on the flank, but only for a moment. Your purpose during this phase is to practice repetitions

to develop an association with the cue on the flank.

Keep in mind that you will re-cue a dog on the Whoa Post after the initial cue on the flank only if he moves. Don't re-cue for head movement or because you think your dog is not paying attention. Often your dog is paying more attention than you realize, and if your dog is standing still and compliant, sending a re-cue only creates mixed signals and therefore creates undue stress on the dog. Remember that you are using the Whoa Post to create a response wherein your dog stands still when cued on the flank. One cue is sufficient, unless your dog makes an infraction and moves after a cue.

During the latter part of the Association Phase, each Whoa Post requires almost a two-part session. At this point, bring your dog to the end of the rope each time and cue as normal, but don't immediately release your dog and move on to the next post after you gain an acknowledgment. Instead, after the acknowledgment, gently pick up your dog and set him back on the ground a foot or so behind where he was, creating extra slack in the Whoa Post rope. This reset will give your dog the opportunity to make his own decision to comply with the previous cue to stand still. The first few times your dog feels the rope go completely slack, he is likely to move forward as if he has been released. As he makes this infraction, re-cue him, and continue as normal. After a few sessions your dog will realize that being set back with a loose rope is not the same as a release and that, since he has not been released, he should continue to stand still. Your dog must come to understand that he was cued to stand still, and he should not move until released with a touch on the head. The rope is no longer holding him physically in place—he is now learning to make the decision to stand still on his own. This stage builds a strong understanding that once cued, your dog should not move on his own until you have released him.

During this stage, it is good practice to add a bit of distraction. Begin incorporating more movement and energy in to your sessions. This in essence increases the challenge and therefore the learning. This provides added opportunity to build on your dog's understanding and abilities to stand still. Walk

toward your dog after he has given an acknowledgment; if he moves, re-cue and walk back toward the end of the rope. Repeat this at different Whoa Posts until you are able to walk all the way back to your dog without him exhibiting any movement. Give him a good, relaxing rub and walk away again; if he follows, re-cue. As his proficiency increases and it is harder and harder to get him to make a mistake, change things up. Use your imagination to think of situations in life and in the field that you would want your dog to be successful at standing still through. Walk in front of him as if you were flushing a bird. Walk to him and touch his collar as if adjusting it. Always have your check cord in hand and the slack out of it, so that you can re-cue in a timely manner if and when he makes a mistake. Don't walk behind him, because it is impossible to correctly re-cue for an infraction when you are standing behind the dog.

One caveat that we would like to emphasize is: Do not use birds as a distraction while working your dog on the Whoa Post. There are myriad reasons why the presence of birds create a bad scenario—the primary reason being that a dog will often lunge forward at the sight of a bird and overstimulate himself. The overstimulation will cause him to back up or bounce back, and voilà! You've taught your dog to move backwards on birds, and this is not an ideal response.

The Transition Phase is the very last phase of the Whoa Post progression. This phase should only be undertaken when you are confident that you and your dog have achieved complete association with the stimulation on the flank. It is quite likely that the required degree of association will take more than 40 Whoa Posts, but repetition alone is not a sufficient indicator of progress. You are ready for the Transition Phase when the following conditions are in place:

1) Your dog has completed 40 or more Whoa Posts.

2) Your dog does not want to move forward when set back after a cue.

3) Your dog quickly acknowledges after every Whoa Post.

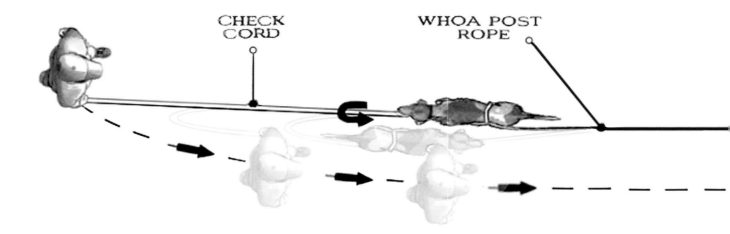

CHECK CORD   **WHOA POST ROPE**

The Transition Phase is your first opportunity to stop your moving dog using a cue on the flank. After completing a typical Whoa Post, simply go to your dog, hold the check cord close to your dog so that he does not lunge ahead of you, and lead him to the opposite side of the Whoa Post. Allow the Whoa Post rope to cue him to stop once he reaches the opposite side.

4) Your dog remains relaxed and confident through each Whoa Post session.

The Transition Phase is your first opportunity to practice stopping your dog while he is moving. This essentially starts as a normal Whoa Post exercise. Check-cord your dog to the Whoa Post, hook him up to the Whoa Post rope, and bring him to the end of the Whoa Post rope to cue him. After gaining an acknowledgment, rather than unhooking and check-cording on to the next post, lead him 180 degrees across the post to the opposite side, essentially going from one edge of the Whoa Post straight across to the other. To accomplish this, your dog must travel in a straight line from 6 o'clock on the clock face to 12 o'clock. Be sure to keep your dog beside you in almost a heeling position when moving across to the other side. As your dog approaches the end of the rope, you will have the opportunity to cue again and stop your dog while you are still moving. By keeping your dog by your side, you will be able to time the cue as he approaches the end of the rope,

and you will be able to seamlessly walk on past him.

Be sure to do no more than one transition stop per Whoa Post at this level. Do not crisscross the Whoa Post area, stopping your dog each time. This will simply leave you with a tight-minded dog that has place association. Once you have done one transition post successfully, remove your dog from the Whoa Post as normal, release with a touch on the head, and check-cord away, cuing the dog to move off in a quartering motion as established in the check-cording drills.. The Transition Phase only lasts between three to nine posts. When your dog does not want to move across the Whoa Post area to the transition stop, you have utilized all of the training that is possible with the Whoa Post tool. You are now done with the Whoa Post forever.

You and your dog are now ready to move to the Intermediate Level of Training! This is always a big "woo-hoo" moment for us, as it means that all of the time you have spent working your dog on the check cord has paid off, and things are about to become much more enjoyable for everyone! 🐕

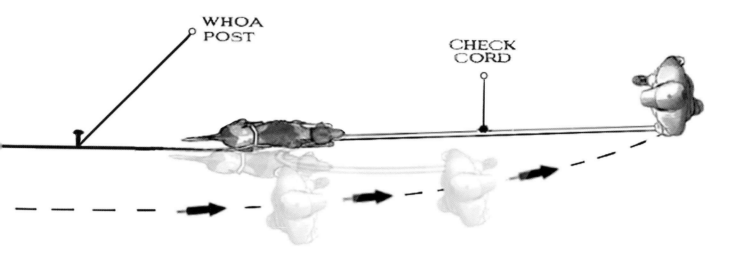

///

GENERAL RULES

The Whoa Post is an essential tool that we use to develop a conditioned response to stand still when cued on the flank. There are a few key points to reference and revisit as you move through the Whoa Post training.

> Be aware that a point of contact on the flank is developed by repetition of cue and release, not by situational awareness of being hooked up to a rope. The dog has to feel a cue every time in order to develop a conditioned response to stop when he feels the cue on his flank.

> Typical signs of acknowledgment may require a bit of practice and awareness to recognize. Look for licking of lips, yawns, big sighs, and repositioning of legs as indicators of acknowledgment.

> Keep your lessons clear and simple. After your dog has been cued to stand, he should stand still until cued to move on.

> Remember, the Whoa Post takes as long as it takes. Don't get bored with the repetition and quit the Whoa Post drill too soon, or you will find yourself fighting an ongoing battle against inconsistent steadiness with a dog that does not fully understand what is being asked of him. Develop a solid foundation for "Whoa" with a clear understanding that a cue on the flank means to stand still, and you will be thanking yourself when you begin steadying your dog in the field!

> When training any animal, confusion is the enemy. Make sure that what you are asking your dog is clear, concise, and consistent so that you do not cause confusion for your dog.

///

*Gently yet firmly guide your dog to success,
go at his pace, and do not overstimulate him.*

THE INTERMEDIATE LEVEL OF TRAINING

Throughout puppy development and the Foundation Level of training, dog and trainer have worked to create a common language of clear expectation and communication, cue and response. To this point, the trainer has maintained a physical connection to the dog by means of a check cord or Command Lead, and all cues have required some degree of contact. The Intermediate Level of training removes the physical connection between dog and trainer, while still communicating the cues that are taught in the earlier stages.

The Intermediate Level begins when your dog is proficient at all of the elements taught in the Foundation Level. This means that your dog has developed conditioned responses to cues, is heeling perfectly on a loose lead, coming to you when when cued, standing calmly beside you when approached, releasing with a touch on the head, quartering smoothly in the field, and have completed the Whoa Post. At this point, your dog should have a high level of prey drive developed through bird exposure in the field, be proficient at using his nose to locate birds, have a high level of intensity on game, be able to recognize a backing situation, and be properly introduced to the report of the gun. If the bird workouts are balanced with the obedience sessions and Whoa Post sessions, all of this usually comes together when the dog has completed the Whoa Post series and is ready to move to remote cues.

If all of this is in place, the fun can begin. Once you have developed conditioned responses to cues, you can introduce the remote cues of the training collar, and you can quickly progress to turning your dog loose in the field, giving him his head a bit more as you work into the steadying process. You can now incorporate the majority of your obedience work into the same field session as your bird work.

TRANSITIONING CUES TO THE TRAINING COLLAR

///

Before you begin using remote cues on your dog, we need to discuss the Smith Training Method's use of remote training collars a bit. First and foremost, our training format tailors the cue of the training collar to the lowest level necessary to gain a dog's attention. At Ronnie Smith Kennels, we think of the training collar as a way of communicating with our dogs at a distance. Because we have spent the time and effort to build a clear foundation, the dog knows exactly what each cue means. It is, again, like communicating via Morse code. Using this philosophy, training collars are a very effective method of communicating with your dog at long distances, allowing you to gain consistent responses from your dog in virtually any situation.

Being able to communicate with a dog that is roaming the countryside is essential in maintaining both a standard of performance and safety. We cannot count the number of times that we have saved a hunting dog's life by using a training collar. It is not uncommon while hunting in South Texas to run across dangerous situations with a hunting dog. We have had countless encounters with rattlesnakes, hogs, javelinas, and even vehicles that could have gone quite badly for the dog had we not been able to cue from a distance with a training collar, thereby gaining control immediately. In more urban environments, collars prove their value when a beloved bird dog takes off across a busy street in hot pursuit of a squirrel. If the dog is wearing a training collar, you can take control of the situation and either stop the dog or turn him. The probability of effectively handling the dog

remotely without a training collar is dramatically decreased because the dog is engulfed in the intensity of the chase and oblivious to your shouting and pleading. When used properly, training collars are a great training tool, and we at Ronnie Smith Kennels hope that we never have to turn one of our prized dogs loose in the field without one on as a safety net. Even our old seasoned hands are not turned loose without a training collar in place for their own protection and safety. We simply care too much for their well-being.

Unfortunately, collars can be used in inappropriate ways, and therefore they can be thought of negatively by people who are not familiar with their proper use. We hope that common sense prevails among bird hunters and trainers when collars are considered and that we, collectively, can use collars for the benefit of our animals. After all, our sole purpose should be to keep our dogs safe and to help them have a good life both in the field and in the home.

Each training collar comes with a handheld unit, or transmitter, and a dog device, or collar. The range and variability of stimulation levels and styles on each unit will depend on the make and model of the collar. We suggest choosing a device that extends a little past the range, or distance, at which you expect your dog to run. Furthermore, we recommend click-incremented collars, with transmitters that will shift levels of intensity at a physical click of the dial. In a training environment, you will want to be able to shift gears on the fly and not have to look at your transmitter to know what level of stimulation you are on. Consistency

is key—as a handler, you want to have the appropriate level of stimulation to gain the appropriate response every time.

TYPES OF REMOTE CUES

There are multiple types of cues that can be used with a training collar: vibration, tone, continuous, and momentary. We use each to our advantage in specific scenarios, and we like to maintain an array of options. At a bare minimum, your collar should have both momentary and continuous stimulation that is broken down into small increments of intensity so that you can tailor the level of stimulation as needed, without large jumps in levels.

As you begin to use your training collar, designate a different type of stimulation for different behaviors. Again, think of your training cues as Morse code. It is a way of communicating with your animal at a distance without spoken language.

We recommend using continuous stimulation for stopping. Think of this as analogous to the use of brakes on a car. To stop a car, you don't tap the brakes, but rather you apply the brakes consistently until the car comes to a rolling stop. Similarly, you don't tug periodically on a horse's bit to stop them. No, both take a consistent cue to bring to a complete halt.

Momentary stimulation should be dedicated to all cues that we use when asking a dog to comply with a cue and keep moving, namely heeling, changing direction in the field, recall, etc. While continuous stimulation sends a cue the entire period during which you hold the button down (up to a measured increment of time), momentary stimulation is typically only delivered for ⅛ of a second, no matter how long the button is pressed. This measured increment of a momentary cue allows there to be a consistent, short cue every time. This short momentary cue cannot be duplicated by simply pushing the continuous button and letting go, so it

is important to remember when to use momentary and when to use continuous so that you do not send confusing messages to your dog.

We are absolute believers that every single time you place a training collar on a dog, you should test it on your hand first. You will want to know if a collar is malfunctioning or if it is possibly delivering a lower or higher stimulation level than the last collar you used. You also will want to know exactly what your dog will experience when you stimulate at various levels. We strongly suggest that anyone who sets out to employ a training collar use common, ethical sense in applying stimulation and in testing equipment.

To test a training collar on your hand, place the prongs on the back of your hand or on your palm, whichever works best for you. Be sure to use the same location every time so that you can monitor levels of intensity consistently. Begin with the lowest level of continuous stimulation possible and slowly work up through the levels of intensity until you can feel the stimulation as a tingling sensation. Get familiar with the stimulation and how it feels. Learn the difference between the feeling of a momentary stimulation versus a continuous stimulation. Pay attention to what happens as you change levels of intensity. As always, use common sense, put yourself in your animal's position, and then apply that knowledge to be a better handler.

As you familiarize yourself with your training collar, you will be able to better recognize why different dogs require different levels of stimulation at different times. Often at seminars, we pass the training collar around a circle of human participants, letting each participant hold the collar probes to their hand with the goal of letting us know at which level they begin to feel stimulation. While we conduct this exercise, the participants are entirely focused on the stimulation of the training collar. Because there are no distractions, stimulation is recognized at the lowest perceptible level; we know that were we to add conversation or other distraction to the situation, it would take a higher level of stimulation to gain a given participant's attention. People who are stressed or otherwise sensitive about feeling the stimulation or who have never felt it before tend to notice the stimulation at lower levels. People who have had experience with training collars and are not in a nervous state of mind do not feel the stimulation until it is at a significantly higher level. Dogs are the same way. A dog that is in a nervous state of mind will typically be cognizant of a very low level of stimulation. When that same dog is distracted it may take a slightly higher level of stimulation to gain his attention. Once a dog is accustomed to the stimulation and is distracted, it will take an even higher level of stimulation to gain a response. The level of stimulation should, of course, start low and be increased to reach the point where the dog can recognize and comply with the cue. From there, the level should be tailored to each specific situation and only be applied at a level sufficient to gain the dog's attention in the specific scenario.

When placing a training collar on a dog's neck, the device should be just snug enough that it makes contact. If placed too loosely on the neck, it may give inconsistent cues and therefore cause confusion. When the collar is placed on the flank, it should be slightly snugger. As dogs begin to move in the field, their stomach muscles contract, causing the circumference of their waist to shrink. If the training collar is not snug on their flank, they will again feel intermittent or even no cue. A pretty good general rule of thumb is to have it snug against the dog with it still being easy to slide two or three fingers under the strap. Again, use common sense to make sure your dog is comfortable.

DETERMINING THE APPROPRIATE LEVEL OF REMOTE CUE

As you begin to work with your dog using a training collar, keep in mind that you will be using the lowest level of stimulation possible to gain compliance with your dog. Watch your dog's reaction every time you give a cue. If your dog's body and behavior do not change when you cue, the dog is not aware of the cue and the next cue needs to be slightly higher to gain an awareness so that compliance is possible. When a cue is timely and at the right level, a bystander watching your dog would think your dog simply made the decision on his own with no assistance from the handler.

Just as with a mechanical cue, *the level of distraction dictates the level of intensity*. Be ready to change levels of your cues to be consistent with your animal's state of mind. Do not get hung up in what number you are on or what level the dog is usually aware of. Watch your dog's behavior. He will tell you whether he is aware of the cue or not. As with any time that you are communicating with an animal, use the appropriate level cue to gain willing compliance and keep the animal in a good state of mind.

INTRODUCING THE TRAINING COLLAR FOR HEEL

Once your dog is heeling perfectly on a Command Lead, he is ready to transition to the next level and begin heeling with remote cues. A dog that is heeling perfectly will walk calmly by your side on a loose lead with his head beside your leg and body parallel to the direction you are walking. He will be comfortable changing speed in time with your movements. You should have to make few, if any, corrections with the Command Lead at this point.

When introducing the training collar for the first time we always begin the transition to the remote cue in the most controlled environment possible. This ensures the dog's success. To introduce the remote cue to heeling, we simply overlay the remote cue with the known cue of the Command Lead. Place the collar fairly high up on your dog's neck, just behind the Command Lead. Hold the end of your Command Lead and your transmitter in your hands. Be sure your transmitter is on momentary, as you will want your dog to continue moving as you cue him to heel. You can now choose to overlay the audible command of "heel" and begin walking, and, if necessary, cue your dog with the lead. If your dog makes an infraction while heeling, use

Practice off lead-heeling in areas with little or no distractions and build up to proficient off-lead heeling in areas with higher levels of distractions, such as the bird field.

the appropriate level of momentary stimulation to correct. Use your Command Lead, if necessary, to overlay the familiar cue with the new cue and guide your dog back to position, thereby accomplishing a successful heel.

As your dog gains proficiency heeling with a training collar in place over the course of multiple workouts, rely less on your Command Lead and more on your training collar to correct infractions. You will soon be able to take the Command Lead off your dog entirely and maintain a consistent off-lead heel. Practice this in an area of no distraction, and slowly progress to maintaining a solid heel in areas with higher levels of distraction. The hardest place for a dog to perfectly heel is in the bird field—this is probably also the most important place for him to be able to heel off-lead. As you and your dog become more proficient, practice heeling in the bird field, so that when you need your dog to heel on a hunt, that tool is available to you.

INTRODUCING THE TRAINING COLLAR FOR CHANGE OF DIRECTION

While check-cording your dog with a training collar on the neck, you can introduce the remote cue of the training collar for changing directions in the field. To accomplish this transition, you can simply overlay the low-level cue of momentary stimulation on the collar before the cue of the rope as you check-cord in your practice area. Make sure to find the appropriate level of momentary stimulation to gain a response based on the level of distraction. Within a couple of workouts, your dog will begin to recognize the meaning of this cue and change direction based on the remote cue before you cue with the rope. This is also a good time to overlay the audible you want to be able to use for handling in the field. In our training format, we use two whistle blasts to have dogs change directions.

In practice, this lesson looks like much of your check-cording to date. Get your dog moving in one direction, cue with momentary stimulation then with the cord, and move off in a different direction. The audible command of whistle blasts should just precede the cue.

INTRODUCING THE TRAINING COLLAR FOR A RECALL

We introduce the training collar for recall in a manner similar to the way we introduced the training collar for change of direction. The recall was practiced to perfection during the Foundation Level of training, so at this level, we are simply transitioning from a mechanical to a remote cue and overlaying a verbal cue onto the perfect behavior.

While you have your dog on the check cord, use low-level momentary stimulation to gain his attention and cue him to you with the rope. You will also overlay the verbal command "here" at this time. Within a few exercises, your dog will come straight to you before you have the chance to cue with the check cord. When your dog responds perfectly every time to the remote cue, you know that you can begin using that cue without the assistance of the check cord.

INTRODUCING THE TRAINING COLLAR FOR STOPPING A DOG

Once your dog has successfully completed the Whoa Post series, transition to the training collar on the flank for stopping is usually easy and seamless. You will begin by check-cording your dog out to the controlled environment where you have done your Whoa Posting and obedience. Beginning a new level of training in a more controlled environment always increases the level of success. For that reason, we do not recommend introducing the collar in the bird field.

As you are check-cording your dog, take a mental inventory of his state of mind. Is he tight, or not moving forward freely and in a relaxed manner? Is he loose and carefree as he travels? How receptive is he to you? Is he oblivious to the fact that you are even nearby? All of these factors give great insight into a dog's mental state and how your workout should progress.

Once you feel that your dog is moving freely and in a receptive state of mind, call or cue him to you and fasten a training collar to his flank. As your dog exercises, his abdominal muscles tighten up and the circumference of his flank will be reduced.

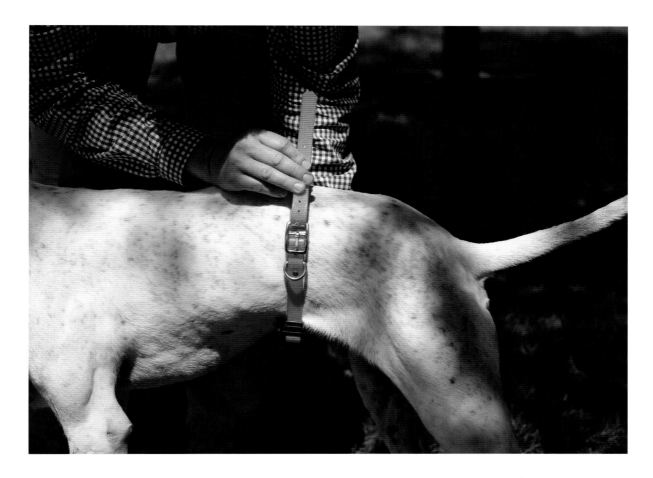

Keep this in mind as you put the training collar on his flank; while he is in the field exercising, the collar should fit snugly at the smallest point on the flank. If you are working a male dog, make certain the collar is placed in front of his genitals. It should fit comfortably just around the flank.

After you have securely fastened the training collar on your dog's flank, he may not want to move. This response is no cause for concern. Place yourself in your dog's position—for the past couple of weeks, you have been teaching him that pressure around his flank means to stop and stand still. By placing a snug strap on his flank, you have essentially cued him to stop. It is actually a very good sign if your dog is reluctant to move once the collar is placed on his flank. It proves that your dog really does have a solid understanding of what was taught on the Whoa Post. Now it is time to make the transition to a slightly different cue. The first

order of business is to free up your dog's movement and get him comfortable moving with the collar on his flank. Accomplish this by cueing him along with the check cord in your hand. Simply go for a walk with him. Provide him with some leadership, showing him that you expect him to move forward with the collar on his flank. If you do so with conviction, he will buy in, and in a few short minutes, he will be moving freely with the collar on his flank. It is absolutely fine in this transition to use the distraction of a walk in the bird field to keep your dog interested and engaged.

Once your dog is relaxed with the collar on the flank, check-cord him back to the open area in which you have been doing your obedience workouts. Remember, you will have the highest level of success by completing any transition in a controlled environment. For this transition, it should be a grassy area or mowed pasture where there are few distractions. As your dog casts past you moving toward the front, hold the continuous stimulation button down on the lowest level possible. Watch your dog's body language carefully and look for any sign that he was aware of the cue. He may just barely slow his speed, he may turn and visually reference his flank momentarily, or he may shift how he is carrying his body. If there is no change in his behavior or demeanor, move up a level of stimulation. Again, hold the button down and look for signs of your dog becoming aware of the stimulation. Continue slowly increasing the level of stimulation by small increments until you see that your dog has become aware of the stimulation or cue on his flank. That is your baseline read on your dog, and that represents the first level of stimulation that your dog feels. It is a good stimulation level to start on when practicing stops.

As you investigate the level of stimulation it takes to communicate with your dog, do not feel pressure to get it done immediately. Just because you cue your dog and he is not aware of the cue does not mean that you have to make him stop immediately. If he does not feel the cue, you can easily release the button, regroup to set him up for success again, and re-cue at the next level.

If your dog indicates that he has become aware of the stimulation but does not slow down immediately, give him a couple of seconds to mentally process how to react. Hold the continuous stimulation button down—you should see him begin to slow down his pace as the awareness increases. When he comes to a full stop, release the button and allow him to stand still for a couple of seconds, then go to him and give him a rub. Next, cue him on the head to release and move on. As he gains proficiency you can have him stand for longer periods and repeat the distraction and hunt simulation scenarios we used on the Whoa Post, such as walking to him and walking away without allowing any movement. If and when your dog makes a mistake and moves, re-cue with a continuous stimulation of the training collar until he stands still.

Set your dog up for success by starting with short, simple stops. As he gains confidence and

starts developing behavior, begin to add in small challenges. With practice, he will be able to stand for longer periods of time. Practice stopping in the mowed training and obedience field until both you and the dog are comfortable and consistent in your behavior and response. From there, you can progress to taller grass and greater degrees of distraction and, most notably, sessions in the bird field. Each transition you make and every time you change the exercise up, expect your dog to have some degree of failure. Set your dog up for maximum success at each level and help him be successful—as he builds expertise at each level and in each new environment, you can start asking more of him during each workout.

While practicing these reps with your dog, the goal is to keep him in a loose, happy, and compliant state of mind. Your dog will tell you if you are over-drilling, overstimulating, or not clear in your cues. Pay attention to him and adjust your daily workouts to keep him in a healthy, compliant state of mind where he is happy to work with you and look to you for direction.

The first time you stop your dog with the training collar in the bird field, keep him on a check cord and practice stopping him three to seven times. Keep in mind that you should have to increase the stimulation level because the level of distraction has increased. In essence, at this point, you have moved from communicating in pointed whispers in a quiet library to trying to shout over the crowd at a football game to convey a message. The excitement is higher in the bird field and there are far more stimuli to take the dog's attention away from the lesson. After a few successful stops, put your dog up and let the lesson soak in until the next day.

After the dog has gained consistency stopping in the field with the remote cue of the training collar and both handler and dog are comfortable with the routine, it is time to make another transition, the transition to steadying your dog up in a backing situation.

AUDIBLE COMMANDS
Up until the introduction of the remote cues, we have not used many audible commands, such as

While practicing these reps with your dog, the goal is to keep him in a loose, happy, and compliant state of mind. Your dog will tell you if you are over-drilling, over-stimulating, or not clear in your cues.

Pay close attention to how your voice sounds as you issue a verbal command. Make an effort to keep your voice clear and authoritative without sounding overbearing. Also, avoid the common habit of repeatedly issuing a verbal command.

verbal cues, whistles, etc. The focus in the Foundation Level was on building behavior and developing conditioned responses. However, in the Intermediate Level, you should be looking for perfect or near-perfect responses to cues and you should have therefore begun transitioning to cues of the training collar. The transition to a training collar marks an ideal time to introduce audible commands to label the perfect behavior that has been established.

At this stage, you can start introducing the word "whoa" for stopping. As you are check-cording your dog, cue him to stop; once he comes to a complete stop, say, "whoa." This process simply allows you to label the perfect desired behavior.

Throughout the Intermediate Level of The Smith Training Method, we follow a similar process using commands such as "here" and "heel" to label those desired behaviors. As you introduce the training collar to communicate a behavior while the dog is still connected to the mechanical teaching tool of a check cord, simply say the word that you want associated with that behavior. As you introduce verbal commands, be aware that spoken words represent additional stimulation to dogs. If you provide a calm yet authoritative verbal command, the impact on your dog will be much more digestible than if you bark or shout the command to him. Raised voices and repeated verbal commands cause undue stress that should be avoided. Give the command clearly once, and that should suffice to label the behavior.

Pay close attention to how your voice sounds as you issue a verbal command. Make an effort to keep your voice clear and authoritative without sounding overbearing. Also, avoid the common habit of repeatedly issuing a verbal command. For example, if you say "whoa," and a dog doesn't stop, do not continue to say "whoa, whoa, whoa, whoa." Simply stop your dog using the collar and make it clean and clear from the dog's perspective. One "whoa" means stop, not 50 "whoas." Remember that in the hunting field, silence is golden, particularly in a guiding scenario—the less noise you make while hunting, the better your successes will be. Practice a judicious use of verbal commands in the training field and everyone will have a better time in the hunting field!

At this stage you can also introduce the audible command of a whistle. Every hunter or handler may have a unique set of whistle blasts they prefer to use. At Ronnie Smith Kennels, we use one whistle blast to release a dog and encourage him to move on, and two whistle blasts to ask a dog to turn. To introduce the whistle on the release, simply begin overlaying a whistle blast when you touch your dog on the head to release. The dog will pick up on this label within a few workouts and will begin taking off with enthusiasm on the whistle blast. If your dog is uncertain whether he should move, give him some remote leadership by clear and confident body movement in the direction you wish him to go. In the early stages, as you walk off following the release, the check cord will bring the dog along with you. When your dog begins to recognize this command and moves off on his own, we can begin using the whistle to release our dogs from a distance while still working on the check cord. This will transition seamlessly to the field.

In the Intermediate Level, you can use the obedience sessions on the check cord to introduce the whistle for turning and handling in the field. As you give the dog a mechanical cue of the rope to turn, simply overlay the audible command of two whistle blasts. We will work on this extensively later in the Intermediate Level while we are working in the field.

FIELD WORK

PRACTICE BACKING SITUATIONS

If at all possible at this stage of your training, use a remote backing dog or a stationary backing dog to build a conditioned backing response. A remote backing dog is simply a painted cutout of a dog on point that can be raised to standing position remotely (via electronics) when the bird dog that is being worked comes into visual range. A stationary backing dog is a cutout of a dog on point that is securely staked into the ground. Either of these tools works with some forethought, although the remote backing dog is far more versatile—and more expensive. If a stationary backing dog is being used, it should be located in such a position that the dog in training can be cast around a physical visual barrier—like a line of vegetation, a building, or a slope of land—to encounter the backing dog at a visual range of 25 to 40 yards.

We do not recommend using a live dog as the pointing dog at this level. Every time a transition is made in training and a new lesson is introduced, the goal should be to keep the environment as controlled as possible and therefore your dog as successful as possible. Always introduce a new lesson in a controlled environment to build success and then increase the degree of challenge. A live pointing dog might break point during this training session, causing the backing dog to move as well, thereby confusing the lesson. Keep the setup as simple as possible for both you and your dog, and manage the environment appropriately, in this case, by using a man-made pointing dog.

Since we introduced the backing situation while working on a check cord at the Foundation Level of training, your dog should recognize a backing situation and understand that seeing a dog on point means that he should stop because there are birds in the area. He may or may not have a natural inclination to back or honor, but he should at least have a situational awareness at this point. Though the backing scenario practiced at the Intermediate Level is fundamentally similar to the backing drill we did in the Foundation Level, we like to bring this scenario to our mowed obedience area when we introduce it with training collar cues. After a successful introduction in the mowed area, we can move the remote backing scenario to the bird field.

As soon as you can tell that your dog sees the automated backing dog, stop him using continuous stimulation of the training collar on the flank and drop your check cord on the ground to drag. Have a friend or assistant walk in front of the pointing dog and flush a pigeon from his or her bird bag. Your dog will most likely be inclined to chase the bird as it flies off. This is to be expected, and it presents you with an opportunity to stop the dog. If you are working with an automatic or remote backing dog, now is a good time to lower the dog back to lie flat on the ground out of sight. This way your dog will not be asked to release while the backing dog is still visible.

The momentum your dog uses as he chases the bird off will determine the level of your cue. If a dog lazily lopes off in pursuit of the birds, we are going to use very low stimulation to slowly cause

Backing is a visually-oriented drill. Stop your dog once he sees the automatic backing dog.

When the bird is flushed, the dog that is backing will be inclined to break and chase.

As the training dog begins to chase, roll him to a stop with appropriate continuous stimulation on the flank.

him to stop. Inversely, if a dog takes off in a hard, focused chase, we will use slightly higher level of stimulation to stop him. During the initial stage of this drill it is okay if dogs move 40 to 60 feet before being stopped. This is the beginning of the steadying process and you do not want to take too much away too quickly.

After your dog is gently stopped and has settled, cue to release. This can be done with a whistle blast, touch on the head, or both. Check-cord your dog out of the backing dog scenario. Keep in mind that after the chase is stopped and the bird is out of the picture, the distraction level is decreased and the level of intensity on your collar should decrease accordingly. The level of distraction at that exact moment determines the level of intensity of any cue.

BEGINNING THE STEADYING PROCESS

After a few sessions in the field working on backing sessions with a training collar, it is time to add a planted bird scenario to the workout and begin the steadying process on birds. At this point, your dog should be stopping easily with a continuous cue of the training collar on the flank. He should be starting to both recognize a backing situation on his own and beginning to honor on his own without having to be stopped. Depending on the individual dog, you may or may not still have him on a check cord to help guide him in the field.

At this stage you can begin planting one bird in the bird field a good distance away from the set-up backing situation. The birds should ideally be planted in remote launchers at this point, because it is imperative that you as the trainer be able to get a bird flushed at a distance in a timely manner. At this stage, continue using homing pigeons, as you want them to fly out of the area and not be caught by a hard-chasing dog. Quail cannot be relied upon to fully exit the scene.

Plant the bird-launcher in a piece of cover that you can easily identify, so that you are able to exactly pinpoint its location as you are check-cording in. The trainer holding the launcher remote has a great deal of responsibility at this level; the bird needs to be released immediately in time to get out

of the scenario should your dog rush in to flush. The two outcomes you want to avoid most at this level are 1) a bird being caught, and 2) a launcher releasing a bird into your dog's face.

In the event that a bird is caught, do not communicate your dismay. Simply take this opportunity to work on a retrieve. A dog catching a bird, while not ideal, is not the end of the world. The situation wherein a launcher releases into your dog's face is far graver. A releaser going off in a dog's face can cause a variety of undesirable outcomes, the most common being fear of birds or fear of the launcher or release, which in turn causes blinking or bubble effect, which we will discuss in detail later. It is always much better to flush a bird early and then realize that your dog never really saw or smelled it than it is to flush a bird too late.

As the bird is flushed and your dog begins to pursue, simply use continuous stimulation on the flank to slowly stop the chase. The goal is to slowly roll the dog to a complete stop. To an outside observer, this should look like the dog simply decided to stop of his own accord. He should slow to a stop, stand still, and watch the bird fly off. You will want to allow him 30 to 40 yards of chase as you slowly stop him during the first few workouts at this level. As your workouts get better and better, the distance and duration of the chase should get shorter.

Remember that you are using continuous stimulation to stop your dog. Do not use momentary stimulation in this instance, as doing so would be like tapping the brakes, and the dog's mind would not change. Also, do not try to stop your dog solely using the verbal cue of "whoa"—it is the cue of the collar that will build consistent behavior. Resist the urge to repeatedly say, "whoa, whoa, whoa" as the dog chases the bird. If you want to overlay the verbal command of "whoa," wait until the dog has stopped and then give a single clear command. That way, yet again, you are labeling the perfect behavior rather than the imperfect behavior.

Over the course of a few weeks, you should begin to see a dog that stands on his own after the bird is flushed. All chase should be out of his mind. He should intensely watch the bird fly off but not

As your dog recognizes a backing situation you can let go of the checkcord and maintain control using the cues established with the training collar.

pursue it. At this point you can begin to "stop the creep," molding his behavior on birds prior to the flush. *Only when a dog has the chase impulse out of his mind and will stand and watch a bird fly off will we ever use stimulation to stop a dog in the scent cone before the flush.*

THE BUBBLE EFFECT

The process to steadying a dog on game begins first with stopping the chase and then progresses to stopping the creep. Again, "chase" occurs when the bird is in the air and the dog is pursuing it. "Creep" describes the dog's forward movement after he has caught scent of the bird, but before the bird flushes.

The traditional methods of steadying a dog on game do not differentiate between chase and creep. The most common perspective dictates that once a

dog indicates that he has caught scent, he should be stopped and not move after that. At Ronnie Smith Kennels, we have found commonly that this can create a "bubble effect" or a protective boundary around a bird that the dog feels he cannot move past. This is particularly an issue with visually-oriented dogs.

Think back to an instance when a puppy has encountered something new or strange, be it a turtle in backyard, a house cat, or a first live bird. The typical response of the pup is to bark, crouch, sit, lay down, or run in circles around the new object. There is seemingly some invisible force that keeps the puppy a bit back from the object until he gains confidence around it—it's an invisible boundary or "bubble" around the object that the pup is not yet willing to penetrate. The pup needs to become

Walk to the front to flush the bird. Flush the bird and gently bring your dog to a stop if he chases.

comfortable and confident with the new object before he can muster the courage to go toward the object and make direct contact with it. This can be a time of high stress for a dog.

Now consider a dog that may not have had a lot of exposure to birds. Due to limited exposure, the dog may exhibit a lack of confidence going in on a bird. If he is stopped as he gains scent, a man-made bubble can begin to develop around birds. If the dog wants to investigate, but gets held back, he may wind up exhibiting the exact same behavior depicted by a puppy investigating a new object: running in circles, flagging, crouching, laying down, and barking. A dog that exhibits this response to birds suffers from what we consider to be a classic case of bubble effect.

Don't get us wrong—not every dog that is

steadied by being stopped in the scent cone will exhibit the bubble effect. However, we work large numbers of dogs, and it is unacceptable in our line of work for us to create a man-made bubble around a bird. Even if one dog out of fifty suffers from bubble effect, those are not acceptable odds for us. Hence, we take the safest route in training to ensure that this bubble effect never becomes a problem for any dog.

By allowing a dog to point and go in to flush without being held back early in the training process, you can both mitigate the possibility of creating a bubble effect and demystify the bird a bit for your dog. A dog learns a good deal by being given the opportunity to flush a bird he has found. By going too far up the scent cone, the dog learns how to work scent to determine how far away he is

The handler's movement gives his dog direction
and shows him where "the front" is and therefore
the area where he should be working.

from the bird. By experiencing what causes a bird to flush, a dog is able to refine his ability to handle wild birds down the line.

Again, think about a young puppy learning to work birds. At first, a young dog will not know that strong scent means the bird is close by and that he should freeze or the bird will flush. The young dog will often catch scent and crash through it without any degree of understanding or finesse. A pup with a portfolio of experience crashing into the scent cone has learned to be more careful while stalking prey, placing more emphasis on the stalk and point.

Bear in mind too that in our contemporary culture, most bird dogs grow up in the home. As a result, they spend a significant amount of their developmental months in the backyard. The only wildlife they encounter on a daily basis are the birds at the feeder or the squirrels running down the top of the fence. All of these encounters are sight- and chase-oriented. There is little to no opportunity in normal development for a young bird dog to learn how to use scent to locate prey. As a result, at Ronnie Smith Kennels, we see a number of dogs that are more sight-oriented hunters than scent-oriented hunters. In other words, these are often the dogs that focus on flushing the bird because they want to see the flush and chase the bird. If you steady this type of visually-oriented dog up by making him stand still as soon as he scents a bird, you often wind up with a dog that stands still, often without much intensity, and quite often flagging (a dog's tail moving back and forth while on point). Traditionally, flagging has been attributed to pressure placed on the animal during training or stress around birds. What we see more commonly today is that flagging indicates that the dog wants to see the bird and engage in their video game-like chase.

To manage this visual orientation, it is important to get the chase out of the dog's mind. This is accomplished by repeated workouts of stopping the dog as he chases the bird. It needs to be done gradually and typically takes us about a month of daily training sessions.

As is the case throughout our training format, what is happening in the dog's mind is more important to us than the mechanics. A dog that stands still while flagging and watching a bird fly off is a dog that is telling us he still has chasing on his mind. Until that dog changes from placing a priority on chasing, he will continue to lack intensity on point and may eventually exhibit other bubble-effect behaviors. The key during this training stage is to take the time to remove the chase from the dog's mind through repetitive bird workouts. After the chase is out of the dog's mind, the pointing instinct will get stronger. Only then will your dog be ready to work on stopping the creep. With the chase gone, the dog will steady far more easily.

HANDLING IN THE FIELD
During the Intermediate Level of training we often run dogs in the field with just a training collar on the flank. Since the collar is on the flank, there is no opportunity to use momentary stimulation to cue your dog to change direction or come to you. With the collar around the flank and the dog ranging, you only maintain the ability to stop your dog. This presents a unique set of challenges if you find yourself working a big-running dog that does not naturally want to go with you.

Historically, trainers taught dogs to handle in the field by nagging them with momentary stimulation on the neck to try to gain compliance and initiate a turn. Through working lots of big-ranging dogs over the course of many decades, we have found that handling a dog with a collar on the flank rather than the neck actually presents a cleaner pathway to developing a dog that will make the decision to go with their handler in the field.

The process of handling a dog with the collar on the flank is as follows:

When working your dog in the field, you want your dog working in a range between 10 o'clock and two o'clock in front of you. When you, as the handler, make a turn, that range adjusts according to your new course of direction. You want to keep your dog in front of you at all times regardless of your directional changes, and you want your dog to move in such a fashion that he does not head back behind you at any point. A dog hunting

behind you is covering ground that should have already been covered, while also placing hunters in a potentially dangerous situation should a bird get up behind or among them. If your dog ranges too far laterally or if your dog lags behind the handler, use a verbal reference—"hup," "ho," two whistle blasts, or the dog's name—to alert the dog to your location and to give your dog the opportunity to move in your direction. If your dog does not acknowledge your verbal reference, simply stop the dog using the remote cue. Once stopped with a remote cue, nearly any dog will stand looking in the direction he wants to go; however, your dog will become curious about what you are doing, and he will eventually look toward you. At the moment your dog looks at you, give the verbal cue to release that you have developed in your check-cording sessions and walk in the direction you want your dog to travel.

There are three common ways in which your dog may react once released: He may move in the direction he wanted to travel originally, he may go with you in the direction you want him to go, or he may remain standing still. In this circumstance your dog has a conscious decision to make. If he decides that he still wants to move off in his original direction, simply stop him again. If he turns and goes in the direction you want him to go, that is great, and all cues should cease as the dog makes the "correct" decision. If the dog stands still, keep moving and occasionally offer some verbal encouragement for your dog to move on. Eventually, all dogs make the right decision to turn and move in

the direction of the handler.

Think of the described exercise as akin to rebooting a computer when there is an issue. When your dog is running, he can easily get in a zone where he is oblivious to what is going on around him and solely focused on running in the direction he chooses. When your dog is stopped, he becomes more aware of his surroundings, and he is able to think more clearly about his choices. Alternatively, when your dog is nagged continually with momentary cues on the neck as he tries to run towards whatever he is focused on, he is not allowed the time to slow down and make a conscious decision.

As you practice this style of handling in the field, it will become smoother and smoother. When your dog goes the wrong way, he gets stopped, turns to look for you, gets released, and immediately moves back to the front. Your dog will quickly pick up on the established boundaries and desired behavior. As a result, you will have to handle your dog less down the line, as he will pay greater attention to where you are in the field, and he will be more "joined up" with you.

When handling your dog in the field, it is important to remember that your dog is using the direction in which you are moving as an indicator to tell him which way he should go. Pick your direction and path in a way that is helpful to him. Notably, never stand still while handling a dog unless you want him to come in to you. Standing still is typically only necessary when looking for downed or marked game or when you are ready to call your dog in and go home. Movement gives your

NOTES FOR THE STEADYING PROCESS

> **Stop the chase first.** Chase occurs when the dog is physically chasing a bird flying in the air. At this stage in a dog's training, do not succumb to the temptation of cueing a dog to stand still if he moves after he has established point. Only stop your dog when he is in pursuit of the flying bird.

> **Stop the creep second.** This is practiced after the chase is out of a dog's mind. Once he has established point, he is not allowed to move in and is stopped with the collar. This is the stage where you can correct for any movement after the dog has made game.

> Using multiple flushes can help steady a dog more efficiently.

> The tail is hard-wired to the brain. If the tail is moving rapidly, the brain is working overtime.

dog direction and shows him where "the front" is and therefore the area where he should be working.

STAGES OF HANDLING:

> Bring an awareness.
> Gain compliance.
> Give direction.

DECIDING HOW STEADY A DOG SHOULD BE

Prior to entering the Intermediate Level of training you need to have decided how steady you want your dog to be on live birds. Bear in mind that in competition, different types of field trials or hunt tests have different parameters of steadiness that need to be followed in order to comply and compete successfully. If you plan on competing, do the necessary research to determine what degree of steadiness is appropriate.

If you plan to steady your dog solely for a hunting application, consider your typical hunting environment and scenario. Do you typically hunt with a group of people whose dogs are not steady? Do you hunt on your own? Are you planning to guide hunts professionally? How dedicated are you to maintaining your dog's steadiness over the course of a season? All these factors will play a role in determining the degree of steadiness to which you hold your dog accountable.

If you generally hunt with dogs that break on the flush, it may be futile to train your dog to remain steady through the flush. It is very difficult for a dog to stand still as other dogs rush about him chasing birds and will take extra help from the handler to ensure the level of steadiness remains. If you hunt on your own and are as focused on shooting as you are on maintaining your dog's level of performance, you may want to consider allowing your dog to break on the shot. This is generally the level of steadiness we recommend for hunters, because it is realistic and functional. A dog that breaks on the shot gets to a downed bird quickly and has an increased chance of retrieving it to the shooter. Furthermore, in not allowing a dog to chase on the flush, your dog's manners will be more likely to stay intact over the course of a season.

If guiding hunters, we recommend that you hold your dog steady to wing and shot. A guide is typically not shooting and therefore can keep his eyes on the dog at all times. A guide will also have the collar transmitter in his hand to make a correction when needed. Guides hunt with different folks on virtually every hunt, and often a guide is forced to evaluate a hunter's safety, etiquette, and ability only during a live hunt. A dog that is steady to wing and shot remains still throughout the entire shooting sequence, ensuring that he stays out of the shooting zones and allowing the hunters to focus on the birds.

The dogs on our guide string generally hold steady to wing and shot. The dogs that we train for clients who are seeking a pleasurable hunting experience are generally steady to wing but release on the shot. Field-trial dogs are trained according to the format that they wish to be competitive in. The steadier you want your dog to remain in the field correlates directly to the amount of time and dedication you are willing to allocate to the maintenance of that level of performance—do not train your dog to be steady to wing and shot if you know you will not maintain that level of performance during your actual hunt. Consistency builds behavior.

Note: Train your dog at the level of steadiness that will be functional in the field.

BEHAVIORS EXPECTED AT THE CONCLUSION OF THE INTERMEDIATE LEVEL

As you wrap up the Intermediate Level of training, expect your dog to have gained proficiency in several disciplines. Foremost, he should stop when cued on the flank without even thinking. Your dog should, through the repetitive workouts of stopping the chase, stand through the flush without needing to be cued. Your dog should back and honor on his own with only the occasional reminder or clarification. He should handle naturally and turn to work in front of you when handled. Your dog should heel perfectly, both on- and off-lead. 🐕

THE ADVANCED LEVEL OF TRAINING: TRANSITIONS

The Advanced Level is a stage of training that is full of transitions and brings together all of the elements of the Foundation and Intermediate Levels. This is when all cues are transitioned to the neck, bird work is shifted from pigeons to game birds, and situations are created to closely replicate hunting scenarios. By the end of this level dogs are at the cusp of learned behavior on birds and are ready for the hunting field.

The Advanced Level of the Smith Training Method is the stage of training that is chock full of transitions. This level of training begins when your dog is steady on game when he has the training collar on his flank. Transition into the Advanced Level when the "chase" and "creep" is out of your dog's mind entirely and he requires little or no correction on birds. At this point your dog should be focused on birds as soon as he is turned loose. He should also be proficient at working scent to locate birds.

At this level, your dog needs to transition from cues on the flank to all cues being on the neck. You should also look forward to moving your bird sessions from a focus on pigeons to the sole use of game birds, which in turn will transition into training sessions during which you will be shooting live birds over your dog. All of the prep work you have done up to this point will help your transitions go smoothly.

It is important to note that often two to three days after you begin any transition, the wheels can, in essence, fall off the wagon a bit. We have watched class after class of students and dogs go through this process, and the cycle of apparent regression is quite common. During the first couple of workouts on new exercises in the Advanced Level, we regularly congratulate ourselves on how seamlessly we have carried the class through the transitions. In these moments, we are quick to celebrate what good trainers we are. Then, almost without fail, little issues begin to pop up with various dogs. We hang our heads, thinking all of a sudden that we overestimated our own abilities and those of our dogs. We then turn our attention to working through the issues, and invariably, we come out the other side of the transition with the dogs looking better than ever.

We share this to say that if you see those bobbles in your own training process through this stage, don't despair. Minor hiccups and setbacks are a normal part of this training process—they do not mean that you have a flaw in your training process or that your dog will never be a success in the field. Keep analyzing your dog's behavior and address each issue by going back a step and reviewing the basics. This is the beauty of a stair-step method such as ours—you can always take a step back, reference what has already been taught, and then move on smoothly to the new lessons.

MOVING ALL CUES TO THE NECK

At our kennel and through our training seminars, we often get asked the question "do you always keep your dog's collar on the flank?" The answer is "Goodness, no!" Once our dogs are standing steady on game in the field and have completed all of the Intermediate Level exercises, we can successfully transition all cues to the training collar on the neck.

To make the transition to the neck, we suggest taking your dog back to the yard. Again, all transitions are more successful in a controlled environment. To easily make this transition, place the training collar on your dog's neck and have him heel beside you on a loose Command Lead. Introduce the concept of stopping with the application of continuous stimulation of the training collar on the neck by stopping your forward movement at the same time you give your dog a low-level continuous cue on the neck. The fact that you are stopping your body and therefore indicating to your dog to stop in conjunction with low-level continuous stimulation on the neck will help introduce this concept in a successful way. Practice a series of these stops during each workout—heel for a while, then cue using continuous stimulation and stop your forward movement to help your dog stop his.

Remember stopping your dog should always correlate to stopping a car. If the wheels are moving, the brakes (continuous stimulation) should be applied at just the amount necessary to stop forward motion.

As your dog gains proficiency, increase the challenge slightly. Begin again by heeling your dog on a loose lead, then without changing your pace or demeanor cue with the continuous stimulation. Watch your dog's body language. When he begins to stop, simply drop the Command Lead that is in your hand, so as to not inadvertently confuse him by also cueing him with the lead, and walk on a few yards. If he takes steps to follow and is therefore not successful, repeat the previous exercise, stopping your body's forward movement on a heel to help him.

> *In the transition to the collar on the neck the goal remains the same as it did with all other exercises; you are looking for calm, relaxed, confident compliance. If you notice your dog is mentally stressed, make a note and take action to address it.*

Within a few short workouts, your dog should have a great understanding that a continuous cue on the neck has the same intended response as the continuous cue on the flank. After your dog can confidently stop each time he is asked from a heeling position as you walk away, progress to cueing while you are check-cording him in front of you at about 12 to 15 feet. Gain proficiency in stopping your dog confidently every time you cue on the neck, then move on to practicing stops in the field with higher levels of distraction. Once your dog has learned to stop easily and confidently with a low level of continuous stimulation on the neck, he is ready to go back to bird work. The beauty is that now you can use the collar on the neck for corrections.

This initial transition to the neck can take anywhere from one workout to a week of practice reps. If your dog has issues to work through, he may require a few more workouts than a dog that comes into the transition with a steady mindset. Don't get caught up in how many times you have practiced each of these transition exercises with your dog—pay attention to his body language and how well he understands the cue. Make sure he has complete understanding of the cue before moving forward in your training exercises.

In the transition to the collar on the neck, the goal remains the same as it did with all other exercises; you are looking for calm, relaxed, confident compliance. If you notice your dog is mentally stressed, make a note and take action to address it. Analyze your dog's state of mind at all times. Is he stressed because you have done too many drills? Is he stressed because you have started at too high a level of intensity with your cues? Is he stressed because his personality dictates that he always requires a bit more time going through his obedience drills? If he is confused, he may need to run loose for a few minutes and take a break to loosen up.

To reiterate, when you take your dog back to the bird field to work planted birds with the collar on the neck, everything stays the same. If your dog moves once he has established point, simply stop him using the appropriate level of continuous stimulation on the neck. He should stop just as he did when the collar was on his flank.

DEFAULT OF RECALL

In your training before beginning our training format, have you used the collar a lot for "here" or recall? If so, don't fret—you are not alone. That said, as you transition to using all cues on the neck, you may find that you have instilled a default behavior to a cue on the neck, which will take an extra step to work through in your training format. You may need to help your dog understand that you are now differentiating between a "here," or momentary cue, and a "whoa," or continuous cue. This will take a little extra effort but will definitely be worth the time investment to correct this default behavior.

This default will most likely show itself when transitioning your dog to stop when on a check cord, particularly when he is a physical distance

away from the handling that requires him to make a decision whether to stop or recall. The physical distance between dog and handler buys the handler some time to adjust and address the default recall. In this situation, as you apply continuous stimulation and your dog begins to come in, do not let up on the cue. Letting up on the cue of continuous stimulation will indicate to the dog that he is doing the right thing in coming in rather than stopping. Stand still, say "whoa" once with calm confidence and when he stops in front of you, back away re-cueing as necessary. If your dog moves, he should recognize the cue to stop. With consistency, the intended behavior will begin to become clear. The important thing here is to not release the cue when he completes the recall, and to not reach down and reward him with a touch when he recalls. These responses will add to the dog's confusion.

Practice to perfection. When your dog is stopping perfectly on cue in the yard, then progress as you would have, had the default recall never existed. Keep in mind, however, that you never fully erase a default behavior; it will always remain in the back of your animal's mind. Be ready to address this unwanted behavior in the same manner if it resurfaces at any point during training.

TRANSITION TO GAME BIRDS
When your dog is standing steady on pigeons and you are having to make very few corrections on bird work with the collar on the neck, it is time to transition your training to game birds. The first game bird that we introduce to our dogs is a pen-raised quail, which we choose mainly because of cost per bird and availability. Source whatever gamebird you can in your area. There may be large game farms within a few hours of your location that you can purchase birds from, or there may be local bird breeders you can purchase from. There are also numerous breeders who will ship live birds overnight provided you have a way to keep and store them. The most important thing at this stage of training is that your game birds are able to fly well and get out of the area once flushed. This ability for a bird to get up and go will make a big impact on the success of your workouts.

Poor scenting conditions or poor-flying birds in the final stages of training can lead to poor proficiency in the dog. Some of the consequences of training with birds of poor quality at this point can be a dog that roots out birds or a dog that lacks a staunch point. Try to evaluate the conditions and the birds to create optimal training situations. If you notice that your dog is not performing well at this stage, assess his behavior to be sure that the reason he is not performing at a high level is situational, and not that he simply lacks a clear understanding of the expected behavior.

When transitioning to game birds, there are multiple ways that you can set up your workout. We use a variety of setups, from tip-ups to releasers to simply releasing birds in good holding cover. At Ronnie Smith Kennels, our philosophy is always that the more controlled the environment, the better. We recommend beginning a transition to game birds by placing the birds in a tip-up or releaser, so that you can be in absolute control of when the bird flushes. Mechanical releasers allow

the trainer to release the bird at a distance, similar to the launcher we used with pigeons in the Intermediate Level of training. From mechanical releasers, we can then progress to tip-ups if desired. Tip-ups allow the trainer to walk in front of the dog and release the bird when they step on the tip-up. The tip-up allows for a more advanced scenario, because there is less metal and electronics in the field to gain the dog's attention. The ultimate goal, of course, is to be able to release strong birds into holding cover and to work your dog in as natural an environment as possible.

TRANSITION TO SHOOTING OVER YOUR DOG

Once your dog has become proficient in locating, pointing, and holding steady on game birds, you have reached the point when he is ready to have birds shot over him. It is important to wait until your dog is steady on game birds before he has any bird shot over him. It is natural for dogs to lose a little bit of steadiness at this stage due to the excite-

As you are working with your dog in training or even as you handle a dog that is going through his first season, it is a good idea to have another person shoot for you. This will allow you to maintain focus on your dog and his performance.

ment of the gunshot and the falling bird. Continue to ask your dog to maintain the same level of behavior as you have all along, and the transition will smooth itself out.

As you are working with your dog in training or even as you handle a dog that is going through his first season, it is a good idea to have another person shoot for you. This will allow you to maintain focus on your dog and his performance. If you are trying to shoot and handle your dog, generally you will be mediocre at both tasks.

When working through this Advanced Level of training, it is important to intentionally change the tempo of your workouts. Without even realizing it, you can quickly get into a set pattern of how long you let your dog stand before flushing, how long you wait before shooting, and how long you wait until you release the dog. Those patterns will show themselves in the dog's performance. If your dog typically breaks on the shot and the safety happens to trip up the shooter, often your dog will break in anticipation. In this scenario, your dog may release on his own at the same time the shot would have occurred. Try to maintain a degree of random timing throughout your bird workouts. Do not be in a hurry to get to the bird, flush it, and shoot. Break each exercise down in to segments to ensure that you and your dog can be successful through the point, the flush, and then the shot.

Practice to perfection. Develop learned behavior in the training field first—after those behaviors are deeply ingrained in your dog, you can transition to wild birds, preserve hunting, or competition.

WORKING WITH A NATURAL RETRIEVE
As you begin shooting birds over your dog, it is time to work with his natural retrieve again. Try to put

yourself in the dog's place as you do so. Remember, if your dog has not been specifically trained to retrieve, then any time he returns his prized possession, he has done so because he wants to, not because he is obligated to. Be a cheerleader and help build his desire to want to bring the bird to you.

A typical behavior that a dog shows on the retrieve is to go directly to the downed bird, maybe pick it up, and then look up at the handler to make the decision of whether to deliver the bird. If your dog decides that he wants the bird more than he wants to give it up to you, he will turn and go the other way with it, or he may just abandon it. If your dog shows some ambivalence, there are some specific techniques that you can use to help persuade your dog to bring the bird in to you.

Often the most beneficial way to encourage a dog to bring a bird to you is to begin walking away. Yes, as counterintuitive as it may seem, walking away from the dog can be a great enticement. The mental process that the dog goes through in this case is somewhat akin what happens when a child finally gets the toy he has wanted for a long time. Giving that toy to another person is not even on the child's radar; he wants to hold the precious toy and play with it and keep sole possession of it. Share? No way. However, by walking away from your dog, you create a mindset shift. Your dog's mind goes from one of possession to one of "Oh, we are moving on. I'll take my toy and go too." His focus shifts from what is in his mouth to the desire to join up with the handler. He will routinely go in the direction that the handler does, and with a little bit of positive encouragement, he will come right on in with the bird.

Once your dog comes in to you, reach down and reward him with a good rubbing. Take your

mind off possessing the bird and it will help your dog keep his mind off of who is in possession of his bird. By rubbing him and calming him first, you can release some of his stress and change his possessive mindset to a positive, fun one. Then, almost as an afterthought, have him give you the bird.

Most retrieve issues are created by a possessive mindset—either the dog's possessive mindset or the handler's desire to possess the bird. Make the behavior the most important piece of the exercise and it will help you and your dog accomplish a successful retrieve.

MANAGING YOUR DOG'S NATURAL RANGE

Every dog has a range that he is comfortable working at in the field. For some big-running dogs that range may be 150 to 300 yards. For some dogs, a natural range may be 50 to 100 yards. The range that a dog is comfortable running is dictated by genetic tendencies and experience. Genetics cannot be modified, but you can create experiences that, in time, will change the range in which your dog habitually works.

The first step in establishing a range with your

dog requires that you are consistent. You will have to learn to be consistent at cueing your dog every time he goes farther than you would like. If you would like to set your dog's range at 75 to 100 yards, then cue every time he crosses that boundary. Don't wait until he is at 250 yards and then cue. Be consistent, so that the range is clear to your dog. Cue with a momentary stimulation and ideally change direction to help your dog join up.

There are three steps to teaching your dog to handle efficiently at any level of training. First, you must supply your dog with an **awareness** of your location and direction. Second, you must gain **compliance** by giving an appropriate cue—either an audible or remote cue, depending on the dog and the situation. Lastly, you must give your dog **direction** by moving off in the direction you would like your dog to move off in.

The most effective way to set a range with a dog is to take the front with angles and teach patterning. "Take the front with angles"…that is typical dog-trainer jargon that might need some translation.

Imagine you have just turned loose your young, hard-running dog. You look up and realize that

according to your GPS your dog is 400 yards ahead of you. If you feel that such a range is way out of bounds and your dog needs to come back in, the simplest thing to do is to cue your dog using momentary, vibrate, or tone to range back in as you continue walking the same direction. Pretty soon he will come at top-notch speed all the way back to you and bounce around at your feet. Great job checking in, right? Not really. Your dog has just perfected a yo-yo. He hunted his way out until he was handled, and then he ran, not hunted, back over the same path to your feet. He bounced around focused on you, his handler, rather than working back in range to the front to find the birds that may lie ahead.

A dog that yo-yoes is a 50-percent hunter. He hunts his way out and retraces his steps back at a dead run. The likelihood of him locating any birds on his return trip is slim, as he has already covered that area and his mind is not on locating game. So how do you shorten a dog's natural range without creating a dog that has a pattern of yo-yoing? "Take the front with angles." When your dog goes past your determined boundary, change directions, and cue him to go with you. Your handling cue can be either verbal, momentary, vibrate or tone. After all, stimulation is stimulation.

Just as in the Intermediate Level of training, if you cue your dog to change directions and he does not comply, simply switch to continuous and stop him. By stopping your dog, you are giving him a chance to "reboot" his computer and make a better decision. By changing direction, you are presenting a "new front" to your dog rather than stopping your dog from going to the front. When your dog changes directions he should angle toward the new front rather than come yo-yoing back to you. When he gets out of bounds in that direction, repeat the process. Dogs pick up on this very quickly and begin to stay in range of their own accord. By handling them in this manner, they quickly get to the point where they need very little handling at all and go with you on their own.

When a dog consciously looks to his handler for direction and willingly and happily goes with his handler without cues, he has "joined up" and is truly part of the team. This is a stage in a dog's career that we believe is critical. When a dog reaches this point, he requires much less handling and, because his mindset is one of confident compliance, everything from bird work to heeling and general manners will greatly improve.

When working to manage a dog's range, balance his natural tendencies with your natural tendencies. If you naturally want a dog within shotgun range and your dog naturally wants to run at about 200 yards, you should probably either meet in the middle or decide it is in both parties' best interest to hunt with another partner. While it is possible to bring that 200-yard dog in to run within shotgun range, it is not going to help that dog's mindset. His instinct will tell him to run bigger, but his team captain will be constantly handling him and working to rein him in. Eventually, resentment and baggage will build on both sides. Try to be the team captain that works with the player's talents and skills. Don't micromanage your teammate—try to develop a relationship in the field in which few cues have to be made, so that a symbiotic relationship rather than an antagonistic one exists.

TEACH A DOG HOW TO EFFECTIVELY HUNT THE COUNTRY

If you have the foundation with which to manage a dog's range and pattern, you can teach a dog to effectively hunt the country that he is in. In tighter country, dogs generally need to shorten up to effectively hunt the cover. In more open country, dogs should range farther to cover more territory. Set boundaries by handling at a consistent range with established, clear expectations of how the dog should hunt the country. Stay realistic about the country and try to not dictate your dog's path by indulging your own fears of losing the dog. Give your dog his head to do his job, rely on your GPS collar in case things go awry, and allow your dog to be what he naturally is.

Work to a level of proficiency where you can allow your dog to work out of sight with the confidence that he is not going to run off, and you know that when he encounters game, he will not intentionally flush it. 🐕

3

///////////////////////////////////

BECOMING A
BIRD DOG

As in any course of education, we at Ronnie Smith Kennels mark the end of the Advanced Level of training with a sort of graduation. Once our dogs have completed this stage, they enter into a place where they can be set free to run on our string as a rookie, showing us what they have learned on the main stage of a real hunt. At this point, we continue to see their progress as an education. That said, they have been given a thorough training in and understanding of what is expected. Now they must enter the hunting field as an adult, to make and learn from the occasional mistakes that come with maturity.

This transition into the rookie year is a magical moment in many ways. It essentially gives us the opportunity to see what a dog is really made of and how they respond to the lessons that wild birds and wild country have to teach. We remain close to steer behaviors or address regressions, but we enter this stage feeling that if we as trainers have done our due diligence, success should be frequent.

Psychologically, this stage is significant. There is an unspoken understanding that the dog has become accountable and is held responsible for doing his part as a member of the working team. We recognize that within that process, we as trainers must relinquish some control of the environment. We are no longer setting out to stage an experience, but rather to place our dogs in a situation where they must act and react, and make choices for themselves. This can be a wonderful, and somewhat nerve-wracking, experience. In the end, however, it is what makes a bird dog a bird dog, and it punctuates a wonderful step in a lifelong relationship.

THE ROOKIE YEAR

This is where the days and repetitions and learning process come together, and the bird dog and trainer enter the field as a working unit.

The rookie year allows the dog the chance to enter an unmanaged environment; to hunt, find, and hold birds in a natural manner; and to learn from whatever ensues. This is in essence the first stage of a bird dog's adulthood, and it represents a big shift in responsibility and opportunity.

TRANSITION TO WILD BIRDS

Our ultimate goal for the dogs on our hunting string is to build proficient wild-bird hunters. We guide on properties around the country that have solely wild birds. We often face challenging terrain and weather, tough scenting conditions, low bird populations, and flighty birds. All of these factors make it difficult for dogs to perform consistently well.

Over the years, the biggest lesson we have learned in maintaining proficient wild-bird finders is that *focus trumps everything*. If a dog is strictly focused on finding birds, he will find more than any other dog, no matter what his level of training or experience. Focus is key. To maintain that all-important focus, we do not worry too much about

manners on birds when we first transition to wild game. We want to build the focus and passion for that scent, and we want to teach our dogs how to work the given type of wild bird in the particular set of conditions that said bird lives in.

The top prospects in our personal string of first-year dogs always accompany us to our northern training grounds to transition to wild birds. The puppies, Rock and Grace, that had joined us in Montana at the beginning of this book went through their formal training the following summer and made the sojourn to Montana that fall to transition to wild birds before earning a spot on our guide string.

Unfortunately, Rock tore a tendon playing with another dog in the exercise yard the first week we were in our training camp. Because of his lameness, he missed a crucial developmental period in his rookie year. There would be many more seasons on wild birds for Rock, but his rookie year would not afford him the extensive experience required to develop an exceptional bird dog at a formative point in his life.

We were crushed to realize that Rock might never reach his full potential just from having played tag with another dog, as any youth would do. His rookie year, the single most important year in a dog's career, would be more about rehab than building proficiency and skill on wild birds.

This, in turn, meant that it was critical for us to ensure that more of our first-year prospects were ready to step into our guide string as top hands. With Rock out of contention for the top spot, his littermate, Grace, slipped quietly into the top rookie position on the string.

On Grace's first outings on wild birds as a trained dog, we went back to the collar on the flank for two reasons: First, Grace's training had taken place months before and while she had been exercised and had received some retrieve work, she had not been worked in the field on birds since the completion of her basic class. Second, Montana training camp represented her inaugural outing as a trained dog on wild birds. To ensure her success in handling this transition, we simply took a step back in her training and referenced the cue developed mechanically on the Whoa Post. No matter what erosion may be created by time off or what confusion may develop during a transition to the training collar on the neck, the foundation developed on the flank is set like concrete and can therefore always be referenced if needed. To make sure any first-year dog is successful in the transition to wild birds, we often go back to the flank for the first workout or two.

As we turned Grace loose from our ATV she ran to the front and stayed there. She worked 100 to 250 yards ahead of us at a ground-covering pace and stayed between 10 o'clock an two o'clock, just

as we had endeavored to teach her in our training pasture back in Oklahoma. Little handling was needed as she checked our progress across the field and continually made the decision to go with us and stay in front. Like most first-year dogs, Grace was not particularly focused on locating game birds. She stopped to investigate different smells and trailed her brace mates occasionally—all well within the norm for any rookie bird dog.

All of a sudden, Grace threw on the brakes and swapped ends like a pro athlete. Her point did not last very long, as her youthful excitement got the best of her and caused her to rush in on scent. She flushed a single sharp-tailed grouse. She followed it for a distance, and then returned to search for more singles. This time, she had a single-mindedness to her actions. Everything in her core was focused on locating more birds. She had just

ABOVE: By allowing Grace a couple of workouts to go through the transition to wild birds, we helped ensure that she quickly became a focused, proficient bird finder.

become a "wild-bird" dog.

By allowing Grace to move in on her first bird contact, we established a building platform for the remainder of her wild-bird experiences. She learned about how to work that type of scent, she learned how close she could get before a wild bird would take flight, and most importantly, she became focused. We did not give any corrections on her performance with that bird and that would pay great dividends in the future.

Unfortunately, that was the only bird located on that brace. However, when we put Grace up in a box, she still had that unbridled fire in her eyes. She was hooked on looking for sharptails. It was

A dog that has experienced a high level of success during his first season is a dog that will never quit hunting, no matter how adverse the conditions are. The experience during the rookie year is what makes a proficient bird finder. It is in that first year that a dog develops a degree of hope, focus, and desire that will carry him through the times when there are no birds.

certainly a successful run, and progress had been made by leaps and bounds.

The next outing for Grace went even better. About 20 minutes into her run, we looked up to see her silhouetted on the sky line, tail and head raised high as if to touch the sky itself. She held point as we slowly made our way toward her with the rest of the brace. Only when we got close and had other dogs backing her did she lose her resolve and charge in. This time, we gently stopped the chase with low continuous stimulation. All of the dogs that were present watched the birds fly off. A successful transition.

On the third outing with Grace, we put the collar back on her neck, and she was focused and standing steady on her birds again. These three simple outings proved to be a small investment in time that paid dividends in her lifetime career. A little extra time ensuring that your dog is successful in any transition is time well spent.

A dog that has experienced a high level of success during his first season is a dog that will never quit hunting, no matter how adverse the conditions are—heat, grass burrs, rocks, cactus, low bird populations, etc. The experience during the rookie year is what makes a proficient bird finder. It is in that first year that a dog develops a degree of hope, focus, and desire that will carry him through the times when there are no birds. Developing this drive is our primary objective with each first-year dog.

As Grace gained proficiency during our month-long training excursion, so did all of her classmates. Each bird contact was better than the last. These dogs still had a lot of lessons to learn in their rookie year, but they were off to a fantastic start as bold, assertive, bird-finding machines.

COMPETITIONS

If you plan to compete with your dog, choose the style of competition you will be entering him in and tailor your training to those rules. Always keep your dog's performance consistent with the rules set by the organization that you are competing in, even if you are hunting and not in competition. Don't change the rules on the dog. If he is supposed to stay steady through the shot for competition, make sure he stays steady through the shot on your hunts. Consistency builds behavior, which in turn wins competitions.

As you prepare for your event, practice the elements that you will be utilizing, but do not just continually train at the competition level. Break it down to work on the individual elements that will make your dog successful. For example, spend separate workouts working on patterning, steadiness, backing, etc. Focus on important requirements of the trial and the weaknesses of your individual dog. Break it down as much as possible and try to build consistent behavior. Consistency is key in getting a dog ready for performance. Practice with the dog's collar on so that you can enforce any behavior necessary. Practice for perfection and go to the trial with confidence. 🐕

There is joy in every moment with a bird dog. Seek that joy, cultivate an appreciation of what each individual bird dog is, and enjoy how marvelous a relationship with a bird dog can be. You will be hooked on bird dogs forever. The journey of training never ends.

WHAT WE HAVE LEARNED

//

We have historically spent the majority, if not all, of our hunting seasons training and guiding on wild birds. Over the decades, we have seen years when the bird numbers were so low, it seemed as if they might never repopulate—and we have seen years when, seemingly out of nowhere, the bird numbers skyrocketed to unprecedented levels. We have seen dry years during which scenting conditions were next to impossible; we have seen years when the cover was so thick it was almost impenetrable; we have seen years when the birds' behavior appeared to be predictable and years when the unexpected became the norm. Over all of the years and all of the days afield, we have narrowed our core beliefs, and have found ourselves relying on a few unimpeachable mantras:

You have to teach a dog how to learn.
Just like people, dogs need an environment that allows them to fulfill their genetic potential. A large part of fulfilling that potential lies in learning how to work through challenging situations to make the right decision. Puppies that are challenged to make decisions at a young age develop into dogs that are better equipped to deal with the challenges of life, specifically the life of a working dog that must adapt constantly to new environments, people, and situations. An engaged mindset lends itself to great behavior.

Every person that comes through a dog's life leaves fingerprints on that animal.
Each of a dog's life experiences stays with him.

These experiences form the lens through which he learns to interpret situations and make decisions. Human interaction with a dog can leave an indelible positive impact—or a negative one. We strive to empower each dog that we put our hands on to become his best self, and we hope that each is better equipped for life due to their experiences with us.

A solid foundation is the building block for life.
Once a foundation is developed in training, it remains in place to help a dog make good decisions. Foundation training may need to be dusted off every once in a while, but the foundation never goes away. It can always be relied upon and revisited.

It takes birds to make a bird dog.
Dogs that experience a significant number of bird contacts during their rookie year tend to be better bird finders for life than dogs that do not navigate that early experience. Keeping dogs working with birds allows them to build learned behavior and proficiency every year. There is no substitute for birds.

Trust your dog.
Give your dog time to work through scent and decipher what he smells. Allow him to work areas of interest to him before whistling him on. He may find birds that surprise you.

Focus trumps all.
A dog that is focused on finding birds will always be the best bird producer, regardless of whether that dog is a seasoned hand or a youthful puppy.

//

Training gives the manners and finesse necessary to keep a dog safe and allow a hunt to be successful. However, without focus, the best-trained dog in the world will not locate many birds. The ultimate bird dog is one that strikes a balance between perfect manners and the driving desire to find game.

If training is not utilized, it might as well never have happened.

It is fairly common for people to assume that since their dog has been through training, he is fully programmed and therefore handling is not necessary. To us that is similar to getting on a horse and never using leg pressure or reining cues. What is the point? If you cannot assist the animal that you are relying on and give him direction and coaching, then you are placing yourself at the mercy of the animal's whims. An undirected horse might just drop his head and graze rather than going in a desired direction or accomplishing any sort of task. An undirected dog might just flush every bird he encounters, chasing each one over the horizon. To comply with our expectations and rules, we need to help our animals by giving them guidance.

What the Future Holds

Formal training provides the cues to enforce behavior and help a dog's performance. A freshly trained "rookie dog" has a good understanding of what is expected, but the teachings have not yet manifested deeply ingrained learned behavior. To reach that level of learned behavior, the dog requires consistent practice. Every dog is different, and the amount of time each needs to become proficient without much assistance from their handler varies. Be patient and consistent. Keep putting your dog on the ground and making sure he gains more experience on birds. He will get better every time.

If you are able to get your dog a lot of consistent experience during his first "rookie season," the next year will be easier and he should be more proficient in all aspects of the game. Remember, it's your responsibility to maintain his focus and performance. Don't let your dog down by not helping him in the field; he will need guidance and cues from you to maintain a high level of performance. Don't forget about him while you are hunting.

No bird dog is perfect. That is part of their marvel and attraction. They are living, breathing, beautifully flawed beings. It is a disservice to think of them as a manufactured product that will perform exactly the same every day once they have had training. Instead of demanding perfection every time, enjoy the relationship, the process, and the experience.

There is joy in every moment with a bird dog. Seek that joy, cultivate an appreciation of what each individual bird dog is, and enjoy how marvelous a relationship with a bird dog can be. You will be hooked on bird dogs forever. The journey of training never ends, and the fun extends for a lifetime.

We hope that this book has served as a tool, illuminating the proven techniques of The Smith Training Method in a functional way while also communicating the philosophy behind it. In the end, we, like you, are folks who love dogs and love to see them shine their brightest.

GLOSSARY

A - E

Acknowledgment: the subtly communicated acceptance of a lesson or a gesture of understanding; dogs acknowledge in all sorts of ways, notably with a softening of the eyes, a yawn, or a licking of the lips.

Anthropomorphism: a human-centered way of interacting with the world by attributing human characteristics to non-human entities, such as dogs

Audible command: any cue a dog can hear, such as a command given by voice or whistle

Automatic backing dog: a mechanical dog silhouette that serves a training tool; the automatic backing dog can be remotely raised or lowered in the training field.

Backing: the act of honoring another dog's point; when a trailing dog sees a dog on point, the trailing dog should stop and "back," ensuring that the pointed bird or covey not be spooked or "busted." This is a visual discipline and not based on the backing dog catching scent.

Bird dog: Vernacular. For the purposes of this book, a "bird dog" is a pointing dog or a dog from the pointing breeds.

Bloodline: genetic breeding record or ancestry; similar to pedigree

Brace: two or more dogs running in the bird field at the same time

Break: i.e. "to break a dog"; traditional term for training an animal

Broke dog: Vernacular. A "broke dog" performs as a fully trained dog and responds with the desired behaviors when handled.

Bubble effect: a distance any animal naturally feels it should stay away from an object of concern; bubble effect may be caused by a lack of familiarity with the object, a negative experience associated with the object, or due to training. Behaviors that may indicate a bubble effect include running in circles, flagging, crouching, laying down, or barking.

Cast: the forward motion of the dog ahead of and at an angle to the handler; a handler may "cast" a dog 45 degrees in front and to the right, and then change direction and cast the dog 45 degrees off to the left.

Check cord: a long (20-foot), stiff lead affixed with a swivel snap to the collar, used extensively in field work drills

Command Lead: Originally created by Delmar Smith, the Command Lead or Wonder Lead is a stiff, 6-foot rope made of a two-strand, wax-coated nylon that creates a simple loop with a hondo, much like a cowboy's lariat. Its spring-like action ensures the dog feels a release from the cue as soon as the handler allows slack in the lead.

GLOSSARY

Conditioned response: an automatic response to specific stimulus established by training; an example is the conditioned response of a dog to stop when cued on the flank. Through training, this cue triggers a conditioned response wherein the dog complies without having to think about how to respond.

Conformation: the externally visible physical composition of a dog, often in the context of a breed standard

Correction: any cue made to enforce a behavior

Crate-training: conditioning a dog to spend time in a crate or dog box

Creep: any forward movement of the dog after he has initially established point, and before a bird flushes — may also be seen in a backing situation

Cue: any stimulation that causes a dog to change a behavior — may be audible, physical, or visual

Cue and release: the cue coupled with the subsequent release that helps a dog identify the correct behavior; a cue of the Command Lead, for example, creates a quick constriction then a release. Upon the release, the dog ideally complies with the desired, indicated behavior.

Dam: the female in a breeding pair

Default behavior: a deeply ingrained habitual behavior

Drag line: a light, stiff cord with no knot at the end which can be snapped to a puppy's collar to facilitate "catching" the puppy

F - J

Field trial: a competitive event at which sporting dogs compete against one another in a simulated hunt situation; there are various types of trials.

Fingerprints: a term used to describe the intended or unintended communication that occurs in every interaction with a dog that leaves a lasting imprint on the dog's behavior and mental state

Flat collar: a flat leather collar that fastens with a buckle, equipped with a D-ring to which a check cord or lead can be snapped

Flush: a bird taking flight or the act of a person or animal crowding a bird until the bird feels it is necessary to take flight

Force fetch: the act of formally training a dog to retrieve; also known as "trained retrieve," this is often employed with dogs that will not retrieve naturally.

"Go with you": term describing the act of a dog joining up and taking direction from the body language or movement of his human counterpart

Gun-shy: a dog that has a negative reaction to the sound of gunfire; often this is a dog that is generally sound-sensitive.

Handler: the person managing the dog's behavior and indicating what commands that dog should follow in the moment

Heeling: the act of a dog, on command, willingly walking beside his handler

Hunt test: Similar to a field trial, but not a competition between or among individual dogs — pointing-dog hunt tests allow dogs to compete against a written standard and progress through a series of levels with given performance requirements.

Join up: *(Vernacular)* the act of an open-minded animal willingly and eagerly looking to a human for direction

K - O

Launcher: a cage that holds a training bird that can be launched in to the air in a timely manner to aid in a quick flush, therefore preventing a dog from catching the bird

Mark: (v.) when a dog visually notes where a bird or dummy lands, or (n.) the actual spot where the bird or dummy lands

Natural range: the range that a dog is comfortable working at in the field without the influence of training

Neutral demeanor: the physical manifestation of a neutral mindset; limited emotion is communicated in posture, tone, and energy.

P - T

Point: a controlled stalk of game

Point of contact: the physical point of contact on the dog's body where a cue is taught

Prey chase: also known as prey drive, the innate desire to pursue moving game, mainly a visual trait

Prospect: a young dog that may eventually make the working guide string or roster

Recall: a command that indicates a dog should return to the handler, also known as a "come" or "here" command

Release: a cue taught to indicate to a dog that he may move forward after being stopped—may be a physical, audible, or visual cue

Releaser: a metal box that holds a training bird and opens to release the bird when a button on a remote device is pushed

Remote cue: a cue delivered by training collar, allowing communication between dog and handler remotely

Scent cone: the invisible path of scent that

emanates from a bird; the scent cone gets wider and less intense the further it gets from the bird in a downwind direction.

Sire: the male in a breeding pair

Socialization: the process of exposing an animal to the environments that he will experience during his life and equipping him to be able to handle those events in a favorable and healthy manner

Stimulation: any action in the dog's environment that causes a reaction; stimulation can be intentional or accidental. It may also be audible, physical, or visual. Stimulation is also the term used to describe the remote cue of a training collar.

Stop the chase: a term used during the steadying process to indicate stopping a dog when it is actively pursuing a bird that is flying in the air

Stop the creep: a term used during the steadying process to describe the process of stopping a dog's movement after it has caught scent of the bird; also describes all movement that the dog makes after the point but before the bird has flushed; may also occur in a backing situation.

Tie-out: the anchored chain and short leads to which one or more dogs can be clipped; a secure way to restrain each dog as it awaits a training session and a great training tool

Tight feet: physical attribute that describes a dog's feet when it has toes that are upright and tight-fitting, preventing undue stress on ligaments and tendons

Tip-up: a wire mesh cage that is placed over a bird to keep it captive during training; when the handler wishes to flush the bird, a metal lever on the tip-up can be stepped on, tilting the cage at an angle up, allowing the bird to flush.

Training collar or e-collar: a collar that transmits a physical or audible stimulation to the dog, allowing the handler to communicate with a dog remotely; may also contain a GPS capability to locate the dog

U - Z

Whelping pen or whelping box: designated pen, container, or other space in which pups are born and spend the earliest stages of life; in this space, the pups are kept comfortable in a safe environment.

Whoa Post: the physical post or stake to which the Whoa Post rope is affixed; the Whoa Post must be rigid and well-anchored.

Whoa Post rope: the rope that comes off the Whoa Post and gets half-hitched around the dog's flank before getting snapped to the collar; must be soft, supple, and comfortable on the dog's flank

ACKNOWLEDGMENTS

This book is dedicated to the pioneers of animal behavior, to the legends who have shaped our training format throughout the decades. Our insights began with the equine knowledge of people like Professor Beery, who shaped the early training techniques of Delmar Smith and Ronnie Smith, Sr., in the 1940s. As horse trainer Ray Hunt himself was known to say, "I'm here for the horse, to help him get a better deal"—these early students of animal behavior inspired all of us to think a little differently and to "be here for the bird dog, to help him get a better deal."

Our training methodology would not be the same without the contributions of our family members. Our training system began with Delmar Smith and Ronnie Smith, Sr.—their understanding of people and dogs bridged a gap in communication and has helped decades of bird dogs and bird-dog owners. Delmar's sons, Rick and Tom, have been instrumental in continuing to modify the system, improving the training and making us all better trainers.

This book is dedicated to the students of animal behavior. We encourage those students to never stop reading animals, to never stop learning from our animal counterparts and to never stop improving training techniques. If we can work with a dog in a manner that allows him to consistently be relaxed and confident in a receptive, learning mindset—then the sky is the limit.

—*Susanna Love and Ronnie Smith, Jr.*

T raining bird dogs has always been a family affair for the Smiths. Through more than 50 years of hard work and dedication, Ronnie Smith Kennels has developed a trusted and proven name in the industry. The Smith family has a history of raising and training fine bird dogs. Ronnie's late father, Ronnie Smith, Sr., was a well-respected trainer. Both Ronnie's uncle, Delmar Smith, and his cousin, Rick Smith, have received the honor of being inducted into the Field Trial Hall of Fame. Bird dogs are not only a business for the Smiths, they are a passion and a way of life.

Ronnie Smith Kennels was started in 1956 by Ronnie Smith, Sr. It is now owned and operated by Ronnie Smith, Jr. and his wife, Susanna Love. For more information, please visit: ronniesmithkennels.com

First published in the United States of America in 2019 by Universe Publishing,
A Division of Rizzoli International Publications, Inc.
300 Park Avenue South
New York, NY 10010
www.rizzoliusa.com

© 2019 Rizzoli International Publications, Inc.
Photography © 2019 Brian Grossenbacher

Text: J. Reid Bryant with Susanna Love and Ronnie Smith, Jr.
Foreword: James A. Baker, III
Photography: Brian Grossenbacher
Additional Photography: Andy Anderson, Susanna Love
Design and Editing: Covey Rise, LLC
Art Director: Laura Buchanan
Designers: Abby Williams, Russ Grimes
Illustrations: James Daley
Production: Mary Katherine Sharman, Addy McDaniel
Copy Editing: Lauren Helmer
Editor-in-Chief: John Thames
Associate Publisher: James Muschett

All rights reserved. No part of this publication may be reproduced, stored in a retrieval system, or transmitted in any form or by any means, electronic, mechanical, photocopying, recording, or otherwise, without prior consent of the publishers.

Printed in China

2019 2020 2021 2022 / 10 9 8 7 6 5 4 3 2 1

ISBN-13: 978-0-7893-3679-8
Library of Congress Control Number: 2019938488

Visit us online:
Facebook.com/RizzoliNewYork | Twitter: @Rizzoli_Books | Instagram.com/RizzoliBooks
Pinterest.com/RizzoliBooks | Youtube.com/user/RizzoliNY | Issuu.com/Rizzoli